CONFESSIONS OF A LAPSED SKEPTIC:

ACKNOWLEDGING THE MYSTERY AND MANNER OF GOD

REVISED EDITION

Todd H. Speidell, Ph.D.

Wipf & Stock
PUBLISHERS
Eugene, Oregon

Wipf and Stock Publishers
199 West 8th Avenue, Suite 3
Eugene, Oregon 97401

Confessions of a Lapsed Skeptic, 2nd Edition
Acknowledging the Mystery and Manner of God
By Speidell, Todd H.

ISBN: 1-57910-234-4
Publication date 3/18/1999
Previously published by Wipf and Stock Publishers, 1999

To Gail and Jessa

CONTENTS

INTRODUCTION

Why believe in God? This perennial question has persisted for me since I grew up in the violent milieu of Paterson, New Jersey, during the 1960s and 1970s. The seemingly academic problems of philosophy of religion—e.g., the meaning of life, the question of God's existence, the problem of evil, and the reality of religious pluralism—have always fascinated me. My purpose in writing this book, then, is personal, not pedantic, even though these abiding issues in philosophy of religion underlie my confessional narrative.

My best friend and ally, Art, accompanied me during my pilgrimage in Paterson. Pivotal episodes from our life together created the case material that I have sketched throughout this book to flesh out the existential issues that we faced together. Our common experiences led him to skepticism and me to faith. I have experienced ample doubt, however, to consider myself a "lapsed skeptic"—similar to some of the skeptical novelist Peter De Vries' characters, who "keep backsliding out of their unbelief, stumbling into Zion, lapsing into faith" (Wood 230). My predisposition to disbelief has mysteriously yet persistently given way to accept the gracious gift of faith from God.

My parents, the Rev. Henry and Mrs. Ruth Speidell, first taught me about faith in God, though it was not until my middle teenage years that their example of faith became more than merely a mark against which to rebel. Their tireless efforts in raising four children in the city while my mother worked as a psychiatric nurse and my father served as a pastor in Paterson abide for me as a memory and a model of faith, hope, and love.

My students at Webb School of Knoxville, believers and skeptics alike, continue to engage me in matters of faith and in questions about God and his relationship with the world. I owe a special word of thanks to Webb students Jennifer Birk, Allison Choat, Hannah Hewgley, Rachel Rhyne, and Emily Serrell for their many helpful suggestions on how to improve the clarity and organization of this book. The appendices comprise cases and stories written by the following Webb Philosophy of Religion students during the 1999-2000 school year: Cara Bingham, Jennifer Birk, Ronnie Bryan, Allison Choat, Ashley Hairston, Maria Lee, Jeff Smolik, and Lisa Stowers. Allison Choat typed and edited this appendix, and I am grateful to her and these other students for their very capable work.

My use of this book in philosophy of religion courses discloses my hope to deepen my daily discussions with students about confessing faith in God. Dr. Chris Kettler of Friends University has been a faithful friend over many years, and his pastoral wisdom and theological insights have both benefited me personally and helped improve this book. I am also indebted to Dr. Kevin Dodd, whose perspicacious and skeptical mind has stimulated me over the many years of our friendship and has helped improve this book. I finally thank Jon Stock and Jim Tedrick of Wipf and Stock Publishers for once again helping me to produce a book that I can use in my classes. Portions of this material have been published in *Christian Scholar's Review* and are reprinted by permission.

As I write this book, I recall how the Church of the Good Samaritan in Knoxville, Tennessee, and Harbour Fellowship in Huntington Beach, California, helped sustain my wife Gail and me when our daughter Jessa was born nearly four months prematurely. She spent her first five months of life in a neonatal intensive care unit and her next several years struggling with her health. We continue to be grateful to these communities of faith that nurture their members through word, sacrament, and deed.

When I look back on the stories and probe the issues in this book, I reaffirm my faith in the self-revealing mystery of God. I do not presume to prove God's existence or goodness to skeptics. Instead, I hope that my musings on faith and doubt will help others reconsider their journeys and obstacles to belief in God.

Chapter One:

Can I Find Meaning in Life?

The only absolute knowledge attainable by man is that life is meaningless.

❖ Tolstoy

I am plagued by doubts. What if everything is an illusion and nothing exists? In that case, I definitely overpaid for my carpet.

❖ Woody Allen

I am the Iceman, fightin' for the right to live
I say better than the glory roads of heaven, better off ridin'
Hellbound in the dirt, better than the bright lines of the freeway
Better than the shadows of your daddy's church
Better than the waiting, baby better off is the search

❖ Bruce Springsteen

At its best our age is an age of searchers and discoverers, and at its worst, an age that has domesticated despair and learned to live with it happily.

❖ Flannery O'Connor

THE CASE OF ART

When Art called upon me Christmas Eve, I knew that it would be a long night. It was the anniversary of Art's stepfather's death, and that signified for Art the loss of his second father (his first father having left home when Art was three years old). And being bereaved of two fathers left Art bereft of hope.

More than once I witnessed Art's stepfather, Ray, berating and bullying Art. More than once, the issue was Art's love of music. When Art was five years old, he began daily practicing the piano for hours. Scales, arpeggios, and classical and original compositions constituted his daily regimen. The explosive exchange that I witnessed on one occasion became an indelible memory: Ray interrupted Art's daily piano practice, violently insisting that Art pursue more "manly" activities. Ray's hardened hands, sullied and strengthened by his blue-collar work, propelled Art across the room. Although I had never before seen such brutality between a father and son, this incident paled in comparison to Art's intervention when Ray hovered over his two biological sons with a steak knife as they cowered in the corner of their bedroom.

Art had bitterly laughed when he initially reported that his tormented stepfather had committed suicide. But when Art arrived at my house one year beyond the reprieve of abuse, the gloomy look on his face bespoke his sorrow that the loss of his two fathers had bequeathed to him.

Woody Allen: Laughing at the Absurdity of Life

In the film *Hannah and Her Sisters*, Mickey (Woody Allen) is a hypochondriac who searches for the meaning of life amidst his fear of sickness and death. Through the character of Mickey, Woody Allen proposes an answer to life's seemingly absurd and pointless nature. Perpetually anguished by the uncertainty and unpredictability of life, Mickey is terrified by the only certainty of life—the inevitability of death. Plagued by his fears and imagined illnesses, he unexpectedly quits his job as a television comedy writer. He then embarks upon a religious quest to avert the ruinous conclusion that nothing matters, since "the only absolute knowledge attainable by man is that life is meaningless" (a quotation by Tolstoy that the filmmaker inserts into his film).

The beauty and certainty of Catholicism initially attract him until a priest counsels a blind leap of faith in lieu of proof. Mickey then tells a Hare Krishna adherent whom he meets on the street that he has abandoned his Jewish upbringing and his momentary attraction to Catholicism and its belief, "die now, pay later." He confesses an attraction to the belief in reincarnation but becomes too anxious about where his soul will actually go—over to another human, or to a moose, or to an aardvark? He finally remarks on Nietzsche's theory of eternal recurrence, "Great. That means I'll have to sit through the Ice Capades again."

His depression deepens. Faced with the prospect of a godless universe, he aims a rifle toward his head but suddenly wonders, "What if I'm wrong?" He insists on the either/or option: certainty or nothing. "In a godless universe," he concedes, "I don't want to go on living." While perspiring and debating with himself, he accidentally triggers the rifle, but the bullet misses him and shatters a mirror instead.

After aimlessly wandering the streets, he meanders into a movie theatre that is showing the Marx Brothers' *Duck Soup*. This film helps put his life back into rational perspective, and he finally realizes the absurdity of life. Considering the worst prospect in life—"there's no God, and you only go around once"—he concludes that he must enjoy life while it lasts and not seek answers to unanswerable questions. He also considers the best outcome—maybe, just maybe, there is a God and an afterlife—however, he concludes that no one can know for sure. Comedy thus enables Mickey to sustain the absurdity of life's struggles.

This newfound realization of the comedic absurdity of life has readied him for a relationship, despite his disappointing first marriage. In the final scene, while reflecting on the resiliency of the human heart, Mickey hugs Holly, who is now his second wife; she in turn informs him that she is pregnant. His commitment to a new wife and their progeny quells his crisis and ends his search (though Allen later criticized his own film as too neat, tidy, and happy in the end, lacking the nerve to recapitulate the Tolstoy quotation on the meaninglessness of life [Bjorkman 156]). The movie commends laughter and love but not faith to cope with the meaninglessness of life. Even in a godless universe, the film concludes, one can create meaning in life.

The lack of faith's certainty plagues Mickey and prevents a leap of faith, given that Allen bases Mickey's quest on the false dilemma of certainty or absurdity. Because he cannot accept what is uncertain, Mickey finally embraces absurdity in the absence of certainty. Allen appears to reject ambiguity (i.e., faith living with, even embracing, doubt) in favor of absurdity (i.e., laughing at the meaninglessness of life).

Walker Percy: Searching for Meaning in Daily Life

The characters in Walker Percy's *The Moviegoer* exemplify the Kierkegaard quotation that introduces the novel: "The specific character of despair is precisely this: it is unaware of being despair." Binx Bolling, the protagonist of the novel, especially demonstrates Kierkegaard's insight by superficially burying himself in his work as a stockbroker and in his hobbies of watching movies and seducing women.

Binx's peaceful though hedonistic existence in suburban Gentilly becomes complicated when he realizes that he has an opportunity to search for a deeper meaning in life, one beyond the hedonism he unconsciously pursues to escape the boredom and malaise of life. "The search," he ruminates,

> is what anyone would undertake if he were not sunk in the everydayness of his own life. This morning, for example, I felt as if I had come to myself on a strange island. And what does such a castaway do? Why, he

> pokes around the neighborhood and he doesn't miss a trick.
>
> To become aware of the possibility of the search is to be onto something. Not to be onto something is to be in despair.
>
> The movies are onto the search, but they screw it up. The search always ends in despair. They like to show a fellow coming to himself in a strange place—but what does he do? He takes up with the local librarian, sets about proving to the local children what a nice fellow he is, and settles down with a vengeance. In two weeks' time he is so sunk in everydayness that he might just as well be dead (Percy, 9f.).

The grip of "everydayness," the enemy of a search, afflicts believers and unbelievers alike. Polls indicate that 98 % of Americans believe in God and 2 % do not, leading Binx to comment that no one searches, undoubtedly because people are "so sunk in everydayness that not even the possibility of a search has occurred to them" (10, 127). Binx's Uncle Jules, for example, conceals his obliviousness to despair by being affable and contradictory. His "victory in the world," Binx comments,

> is total and unqualified. He has made a great deal of money, he has a great many friends, he was Rex of Mardi Gras, he gives freely of himself and his money. He is an exemplary Catholic, but it is hard to know why he takes the trouble. For the world he lives in, the City of Man, is so pleasant that the City of

> God must hold little in store for him. I see his world plainly through his eyes and I see why he loves it and would keep it as it is: a friendly easy-going place of old-world charm and new-world business methods where kind white folks and carefree darkies have the good sense to behave pleasantly toward each other. No shadow ever crosses his face, except when someone raises the subject of last year's Tulane-L.S.U. game (25).

God, for such people, becomes a mere device "for the canny management of the shocks of life" (125).

Binx realizes on the day of his thirtieth birthday that dissatisfaction with life is so overwhelming that "what people really fear is not that the bomb will fall but that the bomb will not fall" (200). Binx's recent recognition of his despair prompts him to reconsider his hedonism. In turn, his Aunt Emily challenges him to turn from his previous way of life to her discouraging moralistic viewpoint. She asks him, "What do you think is the purpose of life—to go to the movies and dally with every girl that comes along?" (198). Her ethical ideals charge him to pursue marriage and medical service. She substitutes duty for pleasure and combines idealism with pessimism in her exhortation to Binx:

> In this world goodness is destined to be defeated. But a man must go down fighting. That is the victory. To do anything less is to be less than a man (45f).

In an apparent capitulation to Aunt Emily's gloomy-looking moralism, Binx forsakes his hedonism and develops a relationship with his neurotically dependent cousin Kate, who tells him that she wants "to believe in someone completely and then do what he wants me to do." She pleads, "Will you tell me what to do?" Binx simply replies, "Sure." She responds,

> You can do it because you are not religious. God is not religious. You are the unmoved mover. You don't need God or anyone else—no credit to you, unless it is a credit to be the most self-centered person alive. I don't know whether I love, but I believe in you and I will do what you tell me. Now if I marry you, will you tell me: Kate, this morning do such and such, and if we have to go to a party, will you tell me: Kate, stand right there and have three drinks and talk to so and so? Will you?

"Sure," Binx again replies (173). He later accepts Aunt Emily's opinion of a meaningful life by marrying his cousin Kate and enrolling in medical school.

Has he ended his search (similar to Mickey's marriage in *Hannah and Her Sisters*)? Has he indeed capitulated to his aunt's commitment to duty over pleasure, converting from his former hedonism to her type of moralism? Although both Mickey and Binx get married, Percy does not portray Binx's newfound duty to his wife and medical career as the resolution of the search. Whereas *Hannah's* protagonist, Mickey, culminates his search in marriage, *The Moviegoer's* protagonist, Binx, continues his search through and beyond marriage. His marriage neither represents the answer to his search nor does it merely become a moral container for his hedonistic impulses.

Where, then, does the search end? The criticism that Percy does not provide "instruction in truth-seeking," or an "explicit" revelation of "the terms of the search," or "fully realized philosophies" that give "the reader the solution to the riddle of life" (Magill, ed., 328) misses the point of being on a search, which *intentionally* avoids providing an explicit answer. (This is similar to the philosophy of Soren Kierkegaard, an influence upon Percy that the reviewer acknowledges but then ignores.) This criticism also betrays a blind spot to the subtle yet significant theological dimension represented by two characters that serve as *signs* of God's grace, however ambiguously these signs are revealed in the modern world.

The first character is a black man walking out of a church on Ash Wednesday. "His forehead is an ambiguous sienna color and pied: it is impossible to be sure that he received ashes," Binx observes.

> It is impossible to say why he is here. Is it part and parcel of the complex business of coming up in the world? Or is it because he believes that God himself is here at the corner of Elysian Fields and Bons Enfants? Or is he here for both reasons: through some dazzling trick of grace, coming for the one and receiving the other as God's own importunate bonus?
>
> It is impossible to say (Percy 205f.).

The second character that serves as a pointer to God's "trick of grace" in the modern world is Binx's half-brother, Lonnie, who is paraplegic. He, like Binx, is also a moviegoer and a searcher. Lonnie dies of a viral infection soon after his fifteenth birthday. Binx does not use this opportunity to provide final answers, but instead alludes to Kierkegaard as "the great Danish philosopher" and reiterates the great difficulty of giving explicit religious answers to today's secular society, which is even more secular than the society in which Kierkegaard lived. Also consider the allusion to the atheistic existentialist Sartre: Binx's mother brings the children to Lonnie's deathbed, "all but Jean-Paul" [209f.]. This allusion again hints at Percy's affinity for the Socratically-based Christian existentialism of Kierkegaard, which shunned giving religious answers to people who, like Uncle Jules, were formally religious but lacked personal faith.

Binx begins unaware of his struggle with boredom and despair as he pursues a hedonistic lifestyle, but as he attains greater awareness, he marries and searches in relationship with another person to move beyond his self-centered existence. In the words of Ecclesiastes,

> Two are better than one,
>   because they have a good return for their work:
> If one falls down,
>   his friend can help him up.
> But pity the man who falls
>   and has no one to help him up!
> Also, if two lie down together, they will keep warm.

> But how can one keep warm alone?
> Though one may be overpowered,
> two can defend themselves.
> A cord of three strands is not quickly broken
> (4:9-12).

Binx grows and achieves a more other-oriented attitude, which allows him to openly receive God's signs and tricks of grace. This becomes apparent when he discusses Lonnie's death with the children, who ask him,

> 'When Our Lord raises up on the last day, will Lonnie still be in a wheelchair or will he be like us?'
>
> 'He'll be like you.'
>
> 'You mean he'll be able to ski?' The children cock their heads and listen like old men.
>
> 'Yes.'
>
> 'Hurray!' (Percy 210).

For the novelist Percy, the search does not end with the pronouncement of a pat answer, the resolution of life's riddles, or an explicit exhortation to faith. The novel, as the theologian Karl Barth says, "should have no plans for educating me, but should leave me to reflect (or not) on the basis of the portrait with which I am presented" (quoted in Updike, 1983, 831). Those whose ears are open can hear Percy's hints of the mystery and ambiguity of God's grace in the modern world.

Ecclesiastes: Seeking God in the Monotony of Life

The author of Ecclesiastes, like Percy, examines the vanity and meaningless of life, for "there is nothing new under the sun" (1:2f., 9). Also like Percy, he refuses to exhort explicitly or directly his readers to faith, focusing instead on examining the realities of life as it is lived "under the sun." Work and pleasure, wisdom and folly, righteousness and wickedness—"everydayness," to use Percy's word—all share the common futility of "chasing after the wind." Power, wealth, and prestige are meaningless (5:8ff.). Not even religion and morality are exempt from his existential analysis: "All share a common destiny—the righteous and the wicked, the good and the bad, the clean and the unclean, those who offer sacrifices and those who do not" (9:2).

Ecclesiastes' critique is comprehensive and incisive: knowledge increases grief (1:18), and the same fate overtakes the wise and the fool, because "all come from dust, and to dust all return" (2:14; 3:20; 9:2). Oppressors perpetrate evils and injustices on the weak and powerless, and the righteous are punished while the wicked are rewarded (4:1; 8:14; 9:11). Even the wise cannot discover the meaning of life or the mystery of God's ways; if they claim to know, they "cannot really comprehend" (8:17).

"In order to be prepared to hope in what does not deceive," suggests Georges Bernanos, "we must first lose hope in everything that deceives" (quoted in Ellul, 47). Ecclesiastes emphasizes the vanity of life to naive optimists and oblivious hedonists alike—and it does so to avert, rather than promote, skepticism and despair. Only a fool presumes to explain the mystery and ambiguity of life. When observing the incongruities of life, finite minds—whether they be theistic or atheistic—cannot comprehend God and his ordering of the world. A person may *apprehend* God only when he or she gives up the futile attempt to *comprehend* God. Ecclesiastes declares,

> [T]he fool multiplies words (10:14)
> Do not be quick with your mouth,
>   do not be hasty in your heart
>   to utter anything before God.
> God is in heaven
>   and you are on earth,
>   so let your words be few (5:2).

We "cannot fathom what God has done from beginning to end" (3:11), yet the author's realistic, rather than pessimistic, conclusion is to enjoy life as "the gift of God" (3:12f.). Conceding that human self-sufficiency is an exercise of futility does not necessarily lead to despair; instead, true wisdom acknowledges both the *reality* of life as finite and the *revelation* of God to the humble that approach him with a listening attitude. Ecclesiastes does not attempt to convince us through logical arguments that God will save us from the problems and riddles of life; instead, the book "leads us to the abyss of vanity, where we have to make a decision": namely, is the meaning of life immanent or transcendent? (Ellul 211ff.; 272f.).

The author of Ecclesiastes proclaims his answer without attempting to prove the reality of God or to lessen the mystery and contradictions of life:

> Then I realized that it is good and proper for a man to eat and drink, and to find satisfaction in his toilsome labor under the sun during the few days of life God has given him—for this is his lot. Moreover, when God gives any man wealth and possessions, and enables him to enjoy them, to accept his lot and be happy in his work—this is a gift of God. He seldom reflects on the days of his life, because *God* keeps him occupied with gladness of heart (5:18-20, emphasis added; also cp. 2:24ff.; 3:9ff.; 8:15; 9:7ff.).

Realism thwarts both naive optimism and nihilistic skepticism. Given the futility of self-sufficiency, one may acknowledge and celebrate a relative enjoyment of life. Although life, full of vanities, is but "a chasing after the wind," such a life is not incompatible with joy. One may accept the relative value of human life and wisdom and enjoy one's life and work as a gift from the hand of God.

"Fear God and keep his commandments, for this is the whole duty of man" (12:13), concludes the author of Ecclesiastes. This may also be the key in the search for meaning and joy amidst the contradictions and uncertainties of life.

CASE STUDY QUESTIONS FOR DISCUSSION

❖ What would the following people say to Art about the meaning of life in light of Art's experiences?

- Woody Allen
- Walker Percy
- The author of Ecclesiastes

❖ What would you say to Art about the meaning of life?

❖ How do the following lyrics from Bruce Springsteen's "Gave It a Name" shed light on Art's experience?

> In the fields of the lord
> Stood Abel and Cain
> Cain slew Abel 'neath the black rain
> At night he couldn't stand the guilt or the blame
> So he gave it a name
> So he gave it a name
> So he gave it a name
>
> Billy got drunk, angry at his wife
> He hit her once, he hit her twice
> At night he'd lie in bed,
> he couldn't stand the shame
> So he gave it a name
> So he gave it a name

So he gave it a name

Pa told me 'Son, one thing I know is true
Poison snake bites you, you're poison too'
At night I can feel that poison runnin' 'round
my veins

❖ See Appendix I (pp. 76ff.).

Chapter Two:

Can I Know that God Exists?

I believe in a God who reveals himself in the orderly harmony of what exists.

God is deep but not devious.

❖ Albert Einstein

With what industrious zeal . . . the speculative philosophers . . . have labored to get a strong and complete proof of the existence of God! But in the same degree that the excellence of the proof increases, certitude seems to decrease.

If God does not exist it would of course be impossible to prove it; if he does exist it would be folly to attempt it.

❖ Soren Kierkegaard

Truth is eternal; knowledge is changeable. It is disastrous to confuse them.

❖ *Madeleine L'Engle*

Our knowledge may include far more than we can tell.

❖ Michael Polanyi

THE CASE OF ART (CONTINUED)

Having graduated from high school and pursued a promising but aborted career in music, Art worked as an emergency medical technician on the overnight shift in Harlem.

Art, an atheist convinced that there were no empirical grounds for belief in God, relied on the scientific method to test, measure, and replicate that which is knowable. "Since God cannot be known scientifically," he announced to me one evening, "God cannot be known. Only weak-minded people need God. Their faith is simply a crutch."

While driving around town late one night, Art suddenly pulled over to administer emergency first aid to a man whose ear had just been severed during gang warfare. Using his shirt to dam the gushing blood of the man's head, Art pushed the man and his severed ear into our car as we sped to the hospital. Since no doctor immediately arrived at the emergency room, Art sutured the man's ear back in place himself.

While leaving the hospital, Art announced again, "Ha! God? No, I rely on myself. That man can thank me and my emergency medical skills—not God—for saving his life."

Woody Allen: Choosing Freedom in a World without God

As noted in the previous chapter, Woody Allen does not acknowledge the existence of God, but instead advocates non-religious means for dealing with life's absurdities. Prominent among these alternatives is Allen's idea that in a godless world, human freedom is key.

In an essay entitled "Mr. Big," Allen depicts a woman who needs to know with "absolute certainty" that God exists and so hires a private detective to find God. "That's right," she says, "God. The Creator, the Underlying Principle, the First Cause of Things, the All Encompassing. I want you to find Him for me." The detective then begins to search for "Mr. Big" (1971, 139ff.).

"Of course there's a you-know-what," asserts the detective's first lead, Rabbi Itzhak Wiseman, "but I'm not even allowed to say His name or He'll strike me dead, which I could never understand why someone is so touchy about having his name said." After listening to the Rabbi's appeal to the omnipotent God of the Bible who delivered the Israelites out of bondage and chose them as His people in exchange for a large payoff ("the old protection racket," he notes), the detective next interviews gangster and avowed atheist Chicago Phil. "There's no Mr. Big," he insists. "I couldn't pass all those bad checks or screw society the way I do if for one second I was able to recognize any authentic sense of Being. The universe is strictly phenomenological. Nothing's eternal. It's all meaningless" (141ff.).

The private eye tries to add it all up at a local pub, but it makes no sense: "Socrates was a suicide—or so they said. Christ was murdered. Nietzsche went nuts. If there was someone out there, He sure as hell didn't want anybody to know it."

The detective poses the possibility to his client that Kierkegaard might have been right, namely, that "you can never really *know*. Only have faith. . . . Don't be so rational." Sergeant Reed of Homicide interrupts their discussion: "You still looking for God? . . . An all-powerful Being? Great Oneness, Creator of the Universe? First Cause of All Things?" "That's right," the private eye replies. "Somebody with that description just showed up at the morgue. You better get down here right away," advises the sergeant. "It's the work of an existentialist. We're sure of that. . . . Haphazard way how it was done. Doesn't seem to be any system followed. Impulse." The detective concludes that life is absurd, which ends the woman's quest for "absolute certainty" (144ff.).

How then does one face the absurdity of life? In an essay entitled "The Condemned," Allen portrays the character Cloquet, who "hated reality but realized it was still the only place to get a good steak" (1980, 9ff.). In this story, Cloquet contemplates whether to shoot the infamous Fascist informer Brisseau. While clutching his pistol, he considers the moral ramifications of his contemplated deed: "By choosing my action, I choose it for all mankind. But what if everyone in the world behaved like me and came here and shot Brisseau through the ear? What a mess!" So he drops the revolver and flees. (Boris, played by

Woody Allen, considers murder in *Love and Death*, asking, "What if everybody acted like this? It'd be a world full of murderers. Do you know what that would do to property values?")

Brisseau is nevertheless murdered, and Cloquet is arrested as a suspect. While in jail, he reflects on whether or not there is still time to convert from atheism, but he decides to "meet my fate alone. There is no God. There is no purpose to life. Nothing lasts . . . Why go through this hollow charade called life? Why, except that somewhere within us a voice says, 'Live.' Always, from some inner region, we hear the command, 'Keep living!' Cloquet recognizes the voice; it was his insurance salesman. Naturally, he thought—Fishbein doesn't want to pay off."

As he ponders these questions, the jailer notifies him that the real murderer has confessed. He is now free to go. "The thought of freedom," Allen concludes, "made him feel simultaneously exhilarated and terrified" (15f.).

Allen's play *God* similarly suggests the necessity of exercising human freedom in a world without God. In this play, Hepatitis, a writer of a play entitled *The Slave*, discusses the ending of the play with the lead actor named Diabetes. When they debate the final scene, another character, Trichinosis, proposes that they call on Zeus (a *Deus ex machina*) to descend dramatically from on high to save the humble, hopeless slave Diabetes. "But if God saves everything," the writer objects, "man is not responsible for his actions." "You wonder why you're not invited to more parties," the actor quips. "I don't accept it," the writer persists. "I'm a free man and I don't need God flying in to save my play. I'm a good writer." But an impressive demonstration of the God machine and a reasonable rental rate convince the writer to use it (1975, 125ff., 143ff., 150f.).

Hepatitis' play begins with Diabetes' declaration, "I don't want to be free . . . I like it this way. I know what's expected of me. I'm taken care of. I don't have to make any choices. I was born a slave and I'll die a slave. I have no anxiety." Freedom is dangerous, continues Diabetes the slave. "If there's a war, who do you think gets killed? The free people. But we're safe because no matter who's in power, they all need someone to do the heavy cleaning" (154f.).

The king enters and asks Diabetes the one and only question, "Is there a god?" When Diabetes says "Yes," the king replies, "If there is a god, then man is not responsible and I will surely be judged for my sins . . . This is the worst possible news." As the king prepares to behead the slave, Diabetes calls upon Zeus, but the God machine gets stuck and the lowering wire strangles him. A messenger reads a telegram, "God is dead. Stop. You're on your own" (170ff. Also cf. The Greek chorus in Allen's film *Mighty Aphrodite*, which calls Zeus, "most potent of gods," for help but only gets his answering machine.)

Allen's essay "My Speech to the Graduates" extends his critique beyond theology to the limits of science for "modern man"—that is, "any person born after Nietzsche's edict that 'God is dead,' but before the hit recording 'I Wanna Hold Your Hand.'" Commenting on a toaster that has not worked properly for years, he ponders, "Are we counting on nuts and bolts and electricity to solve our problems?" He also queries, "And where is science when one ponders the eternal riddles?" (1980, 58f.).

Walker Percy et al.: Responding to Lost Faith

Walker Percy also offers a dual indictment of science and theology. His character Binx reads scientific books such as *The Expanding Universe* and *The Chemistry of Life* as part of his search for meaning in life. "The only difficulty was that," he concludes, "though the universe had been disposed of, I myself was left over" (60). Percy also argues against the pretensions of theology by averring that even if God were proven to exist—even if he presented himself—it would not deliver us from our unacknowledged despair amidst the malaise of modern life (128).

The American novelist John Updike's *In the Beauty of the Lilies* tells of a Presbyterian pastor from Paterson, New Jersey, who capitulates to skepticism. He loses his faith in God, confessing that

> to me it's all become relics, things left over from our childish nightmares, when there's daylight now all around us—this is the twentieth century! I can't keep selling myself and others the opposite of what jumps out at me from every newspaper and physical fact I see. The universe is a hundred percent matter, with the energy that comes in waves out of matter, and poor old humankind is on its own and always has been (61).

"God is a non-factor," he continues,

> all the equations work without Him. Science still confesses to mysteries, of course—the ultimate origins of matter, how life came to arise, and so on. But how the forms of life have shaped themselves, how men came to descend from apes, how the Bible came to be written, along with similar accretions of folklore . . . : all this became terribly clear to me. The universe is a pointless, self-running machine, and we are insignificant by-products, whom death will tuck back into oblivion, with or without holy fanfare (74f.).

One response to the lapsed pastor's grounds for disbelief can be found in Updike's *Roger's Version*, in which theology professor Roger Lambert converses with computer whiz-kid Dale Kohler, who claims that he can prove the existence of God on the computer. The professor responds to him by saying that we need not find God, for *he comes to us* as "the living God, Who moves toward us out of His will and love, and Who laughs at all the towers of Babel we build to Him" (22). A god who could be proven, the professor continues, would merely be a pat answer, a boring and impersonal fact, a helpless and wholly uninteresting contingency, and a mere deduction, not the God who gives us the freedom to exercise faith (24, 93, 235). The boy merely treats God as an object with no voice to speak to us. Quoting the Swiss theologian Karl Barth, the professor proclaims, "There is no way from us to God . . . The god who stood at the end of some human way . . . would not be God" (42).

The Scottish theologian and philosopher of science Thomas F. Torrance provides another response to the lapsed pastor's presumption that faith in God cannot match the scientific prowess of the twentieth century. Torrance perceives a convergence of natural and theological science. Both disciplines, when properly understood, insist that reality is knowable and that the object of knowledge determines the method of knowledge. Any true science, whether natural or theological, assumes that reality is knowable, even though the nature of reality is sufficiently complex to preclude a simplistic reduction to the categories of science *or* religion. Without a basic faith that humans can truly even if not fully understand reality—whether that be nature, God, or other persons—the advancement of knowledge is not possible.

Furthermore, the object of knowledge—not the *a priori* assumptions of the human subject—determines the proper mode of rationality, which is to say that humans need different ways of thinking in different realms of life (Torrance, 1980 & 1984; Henderson 161ff.). C. S. Lewis, for example, discusses the hypothetical example of a scientist who suspects that his wife is cheating on him. How should the scientist *qua* scientist respond? Should he set up an experiment that will impartially verify or falsify his suspicion? Infidelity occurs, but such a neutral, detached procedure to test his wife's faithfulness would undermine the personal nature and faith commitment of their relationship. "Knowledge-by-acquaintance," not blind faith, is the alternative to scientific faith. We trust others because we know them to be trustworthy, even when evidence at times seems to suggest otherwise. The refusal to trust another deeply damages our relationship with the other. A personal relationship requires personal faith, knowledge, and commitment to satisfy the intrinsic "logic of personal relations" (Lewis in Eichhoefer 198ff.).

British chemist and philosopher Michael Polanyi discusses the modern shift from belief as "a higher power that reveals to us knowledge lying beyond the range of observation and reason" to "a mere personal acceptance which falls short of empirical and rational demonstrability." Rejecting this split between faith and knowledge, he asserts that no form of knowledge operates without faith commitments (1962, 266). Scientific advancement, for example, depends not only on formal procedures and criteria but also on "extra-scientific" or personal research interests, questions, and passions. The scientist's "vision of reality . . . should recommend the kind of conceptions and empirical relations that are intrinsically plausible . . . even when some evidence seems to contradict them, and . . . what empirical connections to reject as specious, even though there is evidence for them . . ." (135f.).

All knowledge is personal, Polanyi continues, but it need not be merely objective or subjective. The objectivist, on the one hand, ignores the personal dimension of knowledge (e.g., Bertrand Russell's oversimplification that "belief is true when there is a corresponding fact, and is false when there is no corresponding fact" [quoted on 304, n. 1]). This oversimplification does not acknowledge different ways of thinking and thereby illogically insists on natural tests for supernatural events. If miracles could be empirically verified, however, they would not be miraculous, since natural tests can only verify natural phenomena (284).

The subjectivist, on the other hand, disregards the "universal intent" of knowledge, which is to say the claim to speak about reality (300ff.). The skeptic's claim that the reality of God is not knowable, that doubt is more rational than faith, is itself a statement of faith that advocates the skeptic's own beliefs: namely, that the way to resolve differences of religious opinion is to commit oneself to disbelief (294, 297, 314). "The possibility of error is a necessary element of any belief bearing on reality," Polanyi comments, "and to withhold belief on the grounds of such a hazard is to break off all contact with reality" (315).

A "thoroughgoing skepticism" that attempts to bypass faith commitments is impossible, argues Scottish theologian Trevor Hart:

> A mind genuinely open with respect to everything would, like a box with no sides, prove in the final analysis to be empty, quite incapable of containing anything, even doubts. The more we doubt, the more we are compelled to believe and to trust in order to do so. If we shift the focus of our doubting, then we shift our faith commitments to accommodate the process. By doubting one thing we thereby uphold the claim to truth of another. The very process of doubt itself entails the uncritical acceptance of and reliance upon whole frameworks of meaning, so that far from being an exercise of a purely objective nature it is, like every act of

> knowing, a complex procedure rooted in and founded upon commitments of all sorts, most of them beyond the scope of our awareness . . . To doubt, then, is not to avoid unproved beliefs. On the contrary, such beliefs provide the basis on which doubt is founded, by which it is supported, and in terms of which it is formulated and articulated (58).

Postmodernists also reject the modern notion of science as a detached, neutral method that does not involve personal involvement, and so they provide a final response to the lapsed pastor. Grenz's *Primer on Postmodernism* demonstrates the recent shift in epistemology by contrasting the two *Star Trek* series. The original *Star Trek* series represents the modern person's faith in dispassionate, scientific rationality, which is epitomized by Mr. Spock. *Star Trek: The Next Generation* replaces Spock with the android Data, who "believes he is somehow incomplete because he lacks such things as a sense of humor, emotion, and the ability to dream"; includes crew members "skilled in the affective and intuitive dimensions of human life"; and, unlike the original series that ignores the supernatural, shows an interest in God and matters of faith (9). Science is one but not the only form of knowledge in the postmodern world.

Consider, for example, the much-beleaguered creation vs. evolution debate. On the one hand, literalistic creationists declare the scientific veracity of the biblical account and therefore dismiss evolution as a mistaken and godless theory. On the other hand, atheistic evolutionists dismiss the biblical account as contradictory to modern scientific knowledge, and they profess faith in science as the one true source of knowledge. Both views, however, ironically share the same assumption that Genesis *intends* to speak about scientific matters, rather than acknowledge the distinctive theological discourse of its ancient witness to the God who creates and enters into relationship with his world. That God might create through the evolutionary process provides a more comprehensive account of creation, comports better with the complexity of the world as we know it, and acknowledges different ways of thinking.

The novelist Clyde Edgerton puts the point more simply and directly in his novel *Killer Diller.* The protagonist, Wesley, comments on the two different accounts of creation in Gen. 1 and 2:

> The second version comes in the Bible right after the first version and it says that God created man before the animals—instead of after. Did you know, friend, that there were two different versions? I didn't. What these two versions agree on is that God done it all. What it disagrees on is in what order. This teaches us not to sweat the small stuff. This teaches us that if you believe every word in the Bible is absolutely true like some kind of steel trap, then you believe both of those versions are absolutely true, and if you believe that then you ain't using the brain God gave you and you should be making mud pies or something like that—keeping everything in neat little piles (*Killer Diller* 170).

Acknowledging different modes of rationality or distinctive ways of thinking is a good way for believers and skeptics alike to heed Wesley's caution not to reduce the mystery and complexity of the world into "neat little piles."

CASE STUDY QUESTIONS FOR DISCUSSION

- How would the following people respond to Art's claim that science alone provides true and certain knowledge?
    - Woody Allen
    - Walker Percy
    - T. F. Torrance
    - C. S. Lewis
    - Michael Polanyi

- How would you respond to Art's assertion?

- See Appendix II (pp. 92ff.).

Chapter Three:

Can I Believe that God is Good?

My God, my God! Why have you forsaken me?
❖ Jesus

My Lord, my Lord! What has Thou done, lately?
❖ Woody Allen

And if the sufferings of children go to swell the sum of sufferings which was necessary to pay for truth, then I protest that the truth is not worth such a price.
❖ Fyodor Dostoevsky

[T]he warning against theodicy sounded by the book of Job is a warning all too often ignored.
❖ *Terrence Tilley*

Prove to me that there is a God and I will really begin to despair.
❖ *Peter De Vries*

It's so hard to be a saint when you're just a boy out on the street . . .
It's so hard to be a saint in the city
❖ Bruce Springsteen

THE CASE OF ART (CONTINUED)

Both Art and I were home from college, and Art was in an angry, philosophical mood as we walked around the neighborhood one summer evening. While we were debating whether God exists in light of the terrible sufferings and injustices of the world, the issue became immediate and urgent when we heard a thunderous crack. Before I knew it, Art and I were between a small gang and a boy whose head they were cracking open with a baseball bat, and Art was yelling obscenities at the thug with the bat. Art's impetuous intervention of verbal violence sufficed to avert the death of the boy, and apparently the desire for a speedy getaway spared Art and me from the rage of this gang. Reporting their license plate number to the police secured for us a date in court to testify against the gang members, but the boy failed to appear in court that day. "No justice today," Art commented. "Nor will there be justice in heaven."

Woody Allen: Choosing Personal Responsibility in a World without Divine Justice

Woody Allen's *Crimes and Misdemeanors* probes life in a world without God and responds to Dostoevsky's dictum, "If God does not exist, then all things are permitted." He uses the metaphor of the eye to pose the question: "Do the eyes of God see all?"

Judah Rosenthal (Martin Landau) is an ophthalmologist who corrects others' vision but ironically lacks moral vision himself. He has an affair with Dolores Paley (Angelica Huston). As their "fatal attraction" grows, Jack (Jerry Orbach) counsels his brother Judah that a hit man can take care of this problem. "Jack lives in the real world," Judah concludes. After momentarily wrestling with the morality of murder, he hires a hit man to do the deed.

Ben (Sam Waterston) is a rabbi who possesses excellent moral vision but ironically is going blind. In a daydream, Judah imagines that Ben counsels him to confess his wrongdoing, for the world has a "moral structure" based on a "higher power." Ben believes that God sees what Judah has done, but Judah merely replies, "You live in the Kingdom of Heaven."

In a flashback of his childhood, Judah recalls his father Sol's (David S. Howard) announcement at the dinner table: "The eyes of God see all." Similar to the Solomon of Proverbs, this Sol announces that the righteous shall be rewarded and the wicked punished. "*If* he's caught," retorts Aunt May (Anna Berger). Because she considers evil as evidence that the world lacks a moral structure, she challenges Sol to choose between God and truth. Will Sol believe in God or will he see the world's injustices? Without hesitation, Sol chooses God over the truth of reality.

Clifford Stern (Woody Allen), who describes himself as having "great depth and smoldering sensuality," films documentaries on topics such as leukemia and toxic waste. He, too, struggles with the meaning of life. In his current documentary he interviews Prof. Louis Levy (Martin Bergmann), who is gripped by life's paradoxes. In the shadow of the

Holocaust, the professor ponders why a so-called just and moral God would command Abraham to sacrifice his son Isaac. In light of life's injustices, he cannot find comfort in Ben and Sol's God, who supposedly governs the world justly, or in Jack and Aunt May's "realistic" view that "might makes right." Prof. Levy sees but eventually cannot tolerate the ambiguities of life. His suicide note simply reads, "I've gone out the window."

Crimes and Misdemeanors' multiple characters portray ironic contrasts that refute the traditional doctrine of retribution (i.e., you reap what you sow). The rabbi goes blind while the ophthalmologist gets off scot-free. In fact, Judah not only evades punishment (from God, the state, or even his own conscience), but he also prospers and lives happily ever after, walking off with his wife in the end while feeling no compunction for his crime.

Allen's film, however, does not counsel despair. It suggests that individuals assume responsibility for their actions; otherwise, moral chaos will ensue. Allen responds to Dostoevsky's idea, that in a world without God all things are allowed, by following Camus: individuals on their own must practice moral responsibility. "In the absence of a god or something," Cliff says to Judah, a murderer "is forced to face that responsibility himself," a notion that Judah dismisses as "fiction." But a film clip of Prof. Levy contains the last word and speaks for the writer: "We define ourselves by the choices we have made. We are, in fact, the sum total of our choices . . . It is only we, with our capacity to love, that give meaning to the indifferent universe." Allen strikes once again the Camusian chord: There is no intrinsic meaning to human existence, so humans should defiantly—or humorously, for Allen—create their own meaning in a purposeless world.

Job: Protesting Injustice in a Universe Governed by God

The book of Job challenges the simplistic view of the traditional doctrine of retribution that prevails throughout Proverbs (though its author Solomon is wise enough to recognize exceptions to this rule of life—unlike Sol, who accepted Aunt May's false dilemma that one must choose between God and truth). Allen's view that humanity on its own must confront the meaninglessness of life contrasts with Job, the biblical poet of protest, who also questions whether God justly governs the universe. While Job does not question God's existence or power, he does experience the problem of God's justice with *greater* ambiguity than even the modern filmmaker Allen.

Job, whom God himself describes as "blameless and upright" (Job 1:8), suffers without measure. Although his friends initially come to comfort him (wisely sitting in silence with him, not daring to utter a word), they soon reduce the complexity of his experience to a single formula: Repent of your sins! Assuming the traditional proverbial wisdom discussed throughout the book of Proverbs that the righteous are rewarded and sinners suffer, they infer that the suffering Job must need to submit to God's correction to receive his forgiveness. "Who, being innocent, has ever perished?" (4:7a) queries one of the friends. *If* you repent, the friends judge, then God will forgive you. In a wonderfully ironic twist, God finally commands them, not Job, to repent of their presumptuous folly, and he then accepts Job's prayer and intercession for them (42:8).

Job's friends err in proclaiming timeless truth, rather than addressing their friend in his concrete situation. Displaying a lack of wisdom in their attempt to apply wisdom, they rely on religious clichés. When fools (to use the biblical term) indiscriminately apply Solomon's doctrine, they both distort wisdom and dehumanize people in need.

While Job does begin as the submissive, saintly sufferer who refuses to question God (chs. 1 & 2), sharing the traditional theology of his friends and even rejoicing in his calamity (1:21), he soon complains with a bitter cry: Why was I born? How long can I tolerate these miserable comforters? What have I done to deserve God's chastisement? Where is God that I may accuse him? How may I contend with God himself? Who will take up my cause and intercede on my behalf? (ch. 3ff.).

Job experiences an unbearable tension: the presence *and* absence of God. Job *knows* whom he *accuses*. He sees the ambiguities of life with more depth and torment than his friends, who are quick to resolve the ambiguity. Unlike them (and perhaps Allen as well) he now lives with both faith and doubt. Challenging the limits of human wisdom and asserting the majesty of divine transcendence (ch. 38ff.), God does question Job's presumption to know how God does and should govern the universe. Even though God asks his own questions of Job, however, he never rebukes Job's cry of complaint; in fact, he permits Job's lengthy speeches and vindicates Job over and against the presumptuous theology of his friends.

By way of contrast, Allen's essay "The Scrolls" examines "translated fragments" of Job and other biblical passages—though their authenticity is in doubt since the word "Oldsmobile" appears in the texts. When Job complains to God that he is better off without God, in Allen's re-creation, God only questions but never commends the questioner Job. Also compare Allen's rendition of the Abraham and Isaac story, in which Abraham declares, "The faithful do not question." He prepares to sacrifice his son Isaac until God interrupts him to tell him he only jokingly suggested that he sacrifice Isaac (1975, 22ff.).

The book of Job suggests two insights regarding the problem of human suffering. First, humans must acknowledge the limits of their wisdom. Since Adam, humans have presumed to know the difference between good and evil (Gen. 3:5), attempting to extend the limits of human knowledge. The Greeks learn in order to comprehend, as Abraham Joshua Heschel once said; the Hebrews learn in order to revere. Job finally confesses, "Surely I spoke of things I did not understand, things too wonderful for me to know" (42:3). Believers and skeptics have much to learn from the Hebraic mind, including an epistemology that presupposes humility. "God is silent," Allen remarks; "now if we can only get Man to shut up" (1980, 5).

Secondly, God himself speaks to Job. Even though he confronts Job's presumption, declaring to Job the grandeur of creation, he finally commends Job and condemns the folly of his friends' counsel. God speaks, humbling yet comforting Job by his appearance. Unlike a *Deus ex machina* (a god who is extraordinarily present but ordinarily absent), Job apprehends that God is his God. Beyond any intellectual resolution to the problem of unmerited human suffering, Job repents of his all-too-human propensity to control God with questions or answers and simply acknowledges, "My ears had heard of you, but now my eyes have seen you" (42:5).

Job realizes that he can see God on the underside of life. Sol's simplistic slogan of God over truth forces the sufferer to choose between God and the reality of his or her experience, a choice that Aunt May reasonably argues would favor experience in light of life's tragedies. Job—unlike Prof. Levy, who perceives but cannot tolerate ambiguity—brings his questions and complaints to God.

Job heightens the tensions of *Crimes and Misdemeanors*. This biblical poet and man of exemplary faith questions God himself, who in turn challenges but then commends the one who dares to confront the Almighty. Job thereby enlarges the categories of experience: he can now live with both faith and doubt because God is his advocate. While Allen agonizes over ambiguity, Job embraces both faith and doubt: he continues to believe because of, not in spite of, his protest. He knows whom he accuses.

Archibald MacLeish: Proposing Love as an Answer to Job

In Woody Allen's film *Manhattan*, Isaac (Woody Allen) looks Tracy (Mariel Hemingway) in the eye and observes, "You're God's answer to Job." Archibald MacLeish's *J.B.*, a modern spin on ancient Job, similarly suggests human love as the alternative to the absence of divine justice:

> Blow on the coal of the heart.
> The candles in churches are out.
> The lights have gone out in the sky.
> Blow on the coal of the heart
> And we'll see by and by . . .
>
> We'll see where we are.
> The wit won't burn and the wet smoulders.
> Blow on the coal of the heart and we'll know
> . . .
> We'll know . . . (153).

"It is precisely," MacLeish comments on Job and *J.B.*,

> Job's inability to accept whatever happens which is the spring and source of his agony. He cannot believe that God is just, seeing his own sufferings around him, but neither can he live *unless* he can believe in the justice of God. It is the ancient human quandary: the heart of the human agony. The whole play is an attempt to resolve it. And the play's resolution is the only one humanity has ever found which I can accept for myself: the resolution in and through love (1983, 415).

Flannery O'Connor's understanding that fiction "leaves us, like Job, with a renewed sense of mystery" (O'Connor 184) is an apt reply to MacLeish. Job does not "resolve" the mystery but heightens it: God has more questions than answers, and Job learns to live with ambiguity in the presence of God. Job repents—not surrenders, as Elie Wiesel suggests

(233ff.)—of his presumption to know or resolve life's riddles, and he confesses that "I talked about things I did not understand" (42:3). God's anger at Job's friends suggests that the folly to know, not the right to protest, is the object of God's ire. MacLeish's proclamation of human love (in the face of two world wars, Hitler's and Stalin's atrocities, and so on) as the only acceptable resolution of the age-old problem of evil leaves one with an increased appreciation for Job's wisdom in allowing the mystery of evil to remain unresolved.

The Gospel: Revisiting Job through Jesus

The Gospel further heightens the tension of Job. Jesus on the cross poses the problem with unmitigated intensity: "My God, my God, why have you forsaken me?" Did God close his eyes? Did Jesus' cry indicate that God is so holy and transcendent that he cannot bear to look upon those who sin or suffer? If so, his salvation and comfort for the lost and alienated hinge upon a tragic human figure abandoned by his own Father. Or does Jesus' cry of God-forsakenness underscore God's identification and solidarity with people, especially while they are in need? The psalmist David, in the tradition of Job, originally uses these very words to complain to God (Ps. 22), yet David also praises God as his and Israel's deliverer in the second half of this psalm, just as Job eventually perceives God as his defender. God himself takes up David's cry, Job's cry, our cry of complaint in Jesus.

The Pharisees of Jesus' day form another connection between the Gospels and Job. The Pharisees refuse to interact with outcasts and sinners, and, like Job's friends, they distort truth and dehumanize people. Jesus scandalizes these self-righteous saints by preferring to eat and drink (that is, to have fellowship) with outcasts and sinners. Jesus' truth is *for* humanity. He does not accept Aunt May's false dilemma between God and truth. He intervenes in the lives of the brokenhearted and speaks God's truth on behalf of those in need, so that they might apprehend God in the midst of their agony and despair.

The Gospel presupposes God's forgiving grace and sustaining presence for sinners, outcasts, and those marginalized by the vicissitudes of life. Jesus protects the woman caught in adultery from the stones of self-righteous saints, standing as her advocate before telling her to sin no longer. The prodigal son serves as a paradigm of repentance only because the forgiving father goes out to the son to embrace him and to ground his repentance in the father's gracious and joyous love for his son: "But while he was still a long way off, his father saw him" (Lk. 15:20).

Yes, the eyes of God are on the world, but not merely to see all. For the person in need, God is somewhere rather than everywhere. To use the metaphor of *Crimes and Misdemeanors*, God *sees* the agony and distress of those in need *and bears* their sorrows on his divine heart, as displayed in the life and ministry of Jesus.

C. S. Lewis: Reconsidering the Problem of Pain

The movie *Shadowlands* tells the story of Prof. C. S. Lewis and his encounter with the problem of pain. Early in the story, Lewis the intellectual declares that pain is God's "megaphone to rouse a deaf world," quoting from his book *The Problem of Pain* (93). Lewis is sympathetic to those who suffer, but his logical explanations for the problem of pain and his tranquil existence as a professor shield him from meeting suffering face-to-face. Later in the movie, after meeting and marrying a divorced American woman, he suffers intensely during her painful death. Lewis, like Job, cries out in protest. (This is especially marked in the later version of *Shadowlands*, where Anthony Hopkins' protests grow bolder than the timid protests in the earlier version of the movie). "Why hast thou forsaken me?" he wails with the crucified Jesus in his later book, *A Grief Observed* (Lewis, 5).

Lewis' firsthand encounter with pain leaves him with more questions than answers. He gives up, in fact, the attempt to provide final answers to the mystery of evil. "Can a mortal ask questions," he ponders,

> which God finds unanswerable? Quite easily, I should think. All nonsense questions are unanswerable. How many hours are there in a mile? Is yellow square or round? Probably half the questions we ask—half our great theological and metaphysical problems—are like that (ibid. 81).

"We cannot understand," he concludes. "The best is perhaps what we understand least" (89).

"Evil is an existential matter," Ellul concurs, "rather than an intellectual one." Job, for example, suffers while his friends resolve or explain the problem of evil. Ecclesiastes views evil as another example of the vanity of life. Standing with and for them, God makes himself known to those who suffer, so that they may find personal comfort in him and not merely an intellectual answer (228ff.).

Standing silent before the mystery of God is a good alternative to academic explanations for the "problem of evil."

CASE STUDY QUESTIONS FOR DISCUSSION

❖ How would the following people respond to Art's indictment of God's absence in the face of evil?

- Woody Allen
- The author of Job
- Jesus
- C. S. Lewis
- Ellul

❖ How would you respond to Art's complaint?

❖ See Appendix III (pp. 98ff.).

Chapter Four:

Can I Confess Faith in One, True God?

Dogmatism . . . is the greatest of the mental obstacles to human happiness.

❖ Bertrand Russell

My aunt likes to say she is an Episcopalian by emotion, a Greek by nature and a Buddhist by choice.

❖ Walker Percy

Nor does the actual diversity of forms . . . of personal faith signal the call to any kind of thoughtless, lazy theological pluralism.

❖ David Tracy

Our believing is conditioned at its source by our belonging.

❖ Michael Polanyi

The Bible speaks not only of man's search for God but also of God's search for man.

Unless God asks the question, all our inquiries are in vain.

❖ Abraham Joshua Heschel

THE CASE OF ART (CONTINUED)

When Art met Debbie, he encountered a relationship with a cultural Jew. Despite his atheistic convictions, Art agreed to investigate the Jewish faith, but several meetings with Debbie's family rabbi only had the effect of confirming Art's cynicism. "Jews think that they're right," Art concluded, "just as Christians think that they're right."

Art did not refrain from a grand judgment: "*Both*—make that *all*—religions are wrong!"

Combating Fanaticism and Apathy

Growing up in Paterson, New Jersey, at least afforded me a plethora of professional sports teams to root for. One of the sports highlights for me remains the 1986 World Series between the Mets and Red Sox. I not only like the Mets, but also being a good Yankee fan I hate the Red Sox and pray daily that "the curse of the Babe" will always doom the Red Sox from ever again winning a World Series. (By the time the Red Sox traded Babe Ruth to the Yankees after the 1919 season, they were 5-0 in the first fifteen World Series; since then, they are 0-4.)

While watching game six of the 1986 Mets-Red Sox Series with a friend, I was discouraged that the Mets were trailing 5-3 in the bottom of the tenth, especially since they were down 3-2 games overall in the series. Twice the Sox were one strike away from removing "the curse of the Babe."

My friend and I were eating Chinese food, and my fortune cookie promised that my "luck would soon turn around." Three singles and a wild pitch later, I was celebrating one of the most dramatic comebacks in World Series history. (I am of course referring to that infamous moment when Mookie Wilson hit a ground ball straight to first baseman Bill Buckner, and it rolled untouched through his legs to send the series to a game seven, which the Mets also came from behind to win.)

I jumped in excitement over this unexpected turn of fortune in game six, but my friend's wife responded with displeasure that I would display my feelings so wildly over a sporting event. Now if her response had stemmed from her own passion for the Red Sox, I could have understood her pain. But her condemnation of my fanaticism was based on her own indifference to sports; in her view, it just didn't matter.

Her judgment of me as fanatical and my judgment of her as apathetic represent the two problems of fanaticism and apathy in religious discourse.

Fanatics, on the one hand, equate their beliefs with absolute Truth and believe they have a mandate to convert others to their understanding of the Truth. Equating one's own beliefs with absolute Truth, however, disrespects the divergent views of other conscientious people. Decent and thoughtful people often disagree on complex issues, and each of us is more apt to see clearly if we can hear and learn from others' points of view, even when we disagree with them. Such interreligious dialogue can strengthen one's own faith commitments while learning in a spirit of humility and respect from others with different beliefs.

Presuming to possess the Truth is not only disrespectful to others, but it is also disrespectful to Truth itself. True wisdom acknowledges what we do not know, and that is always a good starting point for beginning to understand God.

While fanaticism poses dangers and disrespect to others and Truth, apathy or indifference poses another set of dangers and a different form of disrespect. In light of the fanaticism, dogmatism, or intolerance of some, it is a tempting alternative to avoid religious discussions, mutually agreeing not to voice the real differences that exist between different faiths.

One way to avoid such discussions is to view questions about God's existence and nature as deeply personal and answers as widely divergent so that one concludes that religious questions have no right or wrong answers, or that all religions are somehow equally true. Knowledge of God, however, is not on the same level as preferences for ice cream. It exceeds the bounds of logic to say that God exists for some but not for others, for God's existence is true or false irrespective of our faith commitments. Also, saying that contradictory religious beliefs can somehow all be equally true glosses over the real and fundamental differences that exist among different religions. In chess, for example, there are correct and incorrect moves and also moves that are more correct than others, so it pays to consider which moves are closer to being correct than others and why.

Tolerance truly implies that there are differences to be respected and tolerated, not to be set aside or dismissed. Treating all religions as essentially the same betrays a subtle form of intolerance: namely, insisting that people who fundamentally disagree with one another are actually in agreement. Interreligous discussion must go beyond shallow pleas for unity with prayers to a generic god and should emphasize instead learning to understand and tolerate where we differ while professing and appreciating one's own faith.

One should celebrate, not conceal, the rich religious diversity that exists in today's world. Balancing the quest for truth with a spirit of tolerance holds passion, conviction, and commitment alongside openness, sensitivity, and humility. Humbly expressing one's religious beliefs and articulating why one believes (or does not believe) in God is a good way to avoid both fanaticism and apathy.

Considering Options in Religious Pluralism

"Pluralism," "inclusivism," and "exclusivism" (also known as "restrictivism" or "particularism") have become common parlance for describing different postures toward the reality of religious diversity in our world. The pluralist argues that the major world religions all provide independent pathways to God, hence prioritizing the concern for tolerance over the quest for truth. John Hick exemplifies this position:

> God is always and everywhere present to us—above, beneath, around, and within us. And when a human being is exceptionally open to the divine presence, he or she has a vivid awareness of God, which is then called revelation (Hick in Okholm and Phillips 34).

The inclusivist shares the pluralist's concern to acknowledge God's saving presence in religions other than one's own but stops short of the relativistic inference that all religions are somehow equally true. Christian inclusivist Clark Pinnock, for example, balances the concerns for the truth of his tradition with a spirit of openness and tolerance toward others by arguing that different religions may play a preparatory role in salvation, which is fully found in Christ alone (Pinnock in ibid. 98). Pinnock's position

> does not claim that God *must* or always *does* make positive use of religion in drawing people. It would be surprising if all religions were equally salvific, given the contingencies and diversities involved. It would be comparable to assuming that all current theories in science or philosophy are equally illuminating—a strange assumption. Furthermore, we are not in a position anyway to say what God *must* do or conclude what God has done before testing the given instance. Surely a given religion might be unusable, owing to the depth of darkness or the severity of bondage in it. It seems wiser to say that God *may* use religion as a way of gracing people's lives and that is *one* of God's options for evoking faith and communicating grace (Pinnock in ibid. 100).

The particularist (a less pejorative term than the more commonly used "exclusivist" or "restrictivist") acknowledges the need to respect other religions but emphasizes the importance of upholding the truth of a particular tradition and recognizing the fundamental disagreements of different religions. Christian theologian Alister McGrath, for example, affirms the uniqueness of God's saving work in Christ:

> There is no place for an intellectual dishonesty that refuses to acknowledge, for example, that Christians worship and adore Jesus Christ as Lord and Savior, whereas Muslims regard the Qur'an as the authoritative word of God and Mohammed as his prophet. Both religions are committed to evangelism and conversion . . . in the belief that they are correct; neither regards their mutual differences as a threat to their distinctiveness. For Islam, Christianity is different—and wrong (McGrath in ibid. 162).

By way of evaluation, a healthy dose of pluralism would benefit those who restrict the mystery of God's saving ways to one religious tradition. An easygoing pluralism, however, can obliterate the fundamental distinctiveness or uniqueness of each tradition and dilute the proper meaning of tolerance, which acknowledges and respects real differences. A faith commitment to a particular tradition need not imply fanaticism or intolerance, but it should entail bearing passionate and faithful witness to one's religious tradition as true.

Particularism does greater justice than pluralism in recognizing the distinctive or unique claims of each religion. It limits, however, the freedom of God's grace and encounters special difficulty with the eternal destiny of those who have not heard the saving message. One can proclaim the truth of one's religious tradition, once again, without equating the truth and reality and mystery of God with the all-too-human and limited perspective of one's faith tradition.

Inclusivism achieves a good balance of affirming the wide scope of God's grace beyond the contingencies of culture, time, and place and upholding the particularity of a tradition's truth claim. God is free to save people in accordance with the mysterious manner of his grace, and yet we are also free to declare as best as we know how others may know God. Knowledge of God presupposes personal trust, commitment, and discernment: standing within a circle of faith, rather than in skeptical detachment from the reality of God.

The Christian theologian Karl Barth underscores the point that the only truth claim of a religious tradition is to point to God's saving grace. By itself, no religion is true. It becomes true only from without, Barth believes, by the gracious revelation of God to humanity in the particular history of Israel, Jesus, and the Church. While Barth professes faith in Christ alone, he does not view Christianity as superior to other religions. In fact, he believes that Christians must first apply God's judgment on religious presumption to themselves. In this sense, the Christian religion is like all others. Particularists set limits or conditions on God's free grace; pluralists ignore the historical particularity of the revelation of God's grace. True religion serves God only by pointing away from itself to God's saving revelation in history (Barth in Hick and Hebblethwaite 32ff.).

Mission theologian Lesslie Newbigin suggests that discussions of religious pluralism wrongly focus on the question, "Who can be saved?"—a question that "God alone has the right to give the answer" (176f.). In the words of Barth,

> we have to think of *every human being,* even the oddest, most villainous or miserable, as one to whom Jesus Christ is Brother and God is Father; and we have to deal with him on this assumption (Barth 53). This much is certain, that we have no theological right to set any sort of limits to the loving-kindness of God which has appeared in Jesus Christ. Our theological duty is to see and understand it as being still greater than we have seen before (62).

Acknowledging the mystery of God within a personal and passionate commitment to a particular tradition leads to a more free and expansive view of God's saving ways amidst the many religions of the world; hence, embracing particularity encompasses commonality. Michael Downey sums up both the inclusivist's concern and the theme of the book:

> Mystery often implies a sense of unintelligibility bordering on nonsense. But real mystery is that which invites and allures us into fuller participation, all the while exceeding our want to grasp it, hold on to it, contain it . . . What is most mysterious is God's superabundant life pouring itself forth, the love of God who gives and gives again but

is never emptied in the giving. This self-giving is at the very heart of who God is. The incomprehensibility of God lies in the utter gratuity of life and love, in God's constant coming as gift (42f.).

CASE STUDY QUESTIONS FOR DISCUSSION

- Given the diversity of religious traditions—and Art's point that this diversity entails contradictory truth-claims—would the following people affirm that one can confess faith in one true God without being dogmatic? Why or why not?
    - Hick
    - Pinnock
    - McGrath
    - Barth
- What would you say?
- See Appendix IV (pp. 115ff.).

CONCLUSION

I'm from New Jersey
I don't expect too much
If the world ended today
I would adjust

❖ John Gorka

Let go into the mystery
Let yourself go
There is no other place to be
Baby this I know
You've got to dance and sing
And be alive in the mystery
And be joyous and give thanks
And let yourself go

❖ Van Morrison

THE CASE OF ART (CONCLUDED)

When the phone rang, Art's was the last voice I expected to hear. I had not heard from him in several years. Since our previous conversation, Art had been divorced and jailed.

Art told me of a near fatal illness that he contracted after swimming off of the Jersey shoreline. His extended hospitalization led to the loss of his highly successful career as a financial consultant on Wall Street. His job loss aggravated an already acrimonious divorce, and failure to make timely child support payments landed him in jail.

After a near death experience and a brief but brutal time in jail, Art now seeks reconciliation with his estranged family, attempting to patch up his wounded life (reminiscent of his suturing an ear back onto the man who was injured in gang warfare).

Is there meaning in life? Does God exist? Why is there evil? Can more than one religion be true? These questions have perplexed the great minds of the ages, and this short book has certainly not resolved these problems by offering final solutions.

Philosophy, however, tutors us in asking proper questions. After a significant measure of pain and suffering, my friend Art began to ask new questions and abandon the old dogmatic questions and answers that seemed right to him in his younger years.

Chastened by life and questioned by God, Art was stripped of his defenses and unmasked of his pretensions. He could now ask anew the childlike question, "Who is God?"

Why believe in God? No single answer can be dispensed as adequate for everyone. Attempts both to prove and to disprove God share the common folly of building "a house of cards" (to borrow Lewis' metaphor [1961, 61]), to which the living God responds with laughter. Theistic arguments for God's existence and atheistic arguments against God's existence each cleverly construct their own Tower of Babel. These futile attempts to grasp God, on the one hand, or dismiss God, on the other, cannot domesticate the mystery and manner of God in the world. The emphasis in this book has been on acknowledging God as the basic mystery in life: One whose meaning for us may be apprehended but never comprehended.

When driving home from summer camp one day, my five-year-old daughter, Jessa, observed, "The sun is following us home."

"It only seems to follow us home," I noted, "but it doesn't actually move; we move."

"But it seems to move," she responded. "Even after we went under a bridge, it was still there on the other side."

"Yes, it seems to move," I again pointed out, "but it is we who are moving, not it."

"Ah," she realized, "it's a mystery. It's like we can't see God, but he sees us. Or we can't hear God, but he speaks to us through people, like our parents."

Her wise words far exceed any profundities that I have perceived and any truths that I might have stumbled across in this book. Learning from the young humbles the prideful adult—and humility is the epistemological prerequisite for apprehending the mystery and manner of God. God sees us and speaks to us. And he permits each of us to ask the fundamental question of meaning in life, "Who is God for me?"

GLOSSARY*

Agnosticism: The viewpoint that human reason cannot ascertain God's existence and, therefore, God cannot be known. Agnosticism sometimes supports the belief that, because there is no irrefutable verification of God's existence, humans should suspend judgment about whether to believe or to disbelieve.

A posteriori: Knowledge or understanding that is learned from experience (the opposite of ***a priori***).

A priori: Knowledge or understanding that is not dependent on sensory experiences—e.g., knowledge obtained with the use of mathematics and logic (the opposite of ***a posteriori***).

Atheism: The assertion that there is no God (the opposition of **theism**). This claim is defended by two major arguments. The first contention is that there is unsatisfactory evidence demonstrating a divine being. The second justification for atheism is that the concept of a perfect God is ridden with inconsistencies and fallacies—e.g., if God is all-powerful and morally perfect, then how can evil exist?

Empiricism: The philosophy that all knowledge originates from sensory, or ***a posteriori,*** experience (the opposite of **rationalism**). Empiricism maintains that, while some concepts might seem not to develop from experience, any observation, conclusion, or belief can eventually be traced back to its origin, which invariably is experience.

Epistemology: A major division of philosophy concerned with the theory of knowledge—that is, the origin, nature, extent, and justification of knowledge.

Existentialism: The contention that humanity is not predetermined by nature or by God; instead, humans choose their own destinies and are accountable for their own actions. Existentialism encompasses both theistic and atheistic versions (Fyodor Dostoevsky and Soren Kierkegaard illustrating the former and Albert Camus and Jean-Paul Sartre the latter). These variations differ on whether authentic human choices entail faith in God.

Metaphysics: A major branch of philosophy that explores the general nature of things, people, the world, and God.

Nihilism: ("*nihil*" in Latin literally means "nothing"). The philosophy of denial and contradiction: all endeavors to discover meaning in life eventually lead to nothing. Thus, because it is impossible to achieve a meaningful life, human life is purposeless and empty and skepticism is inescapable.

Objectivism: The viewpoint that some things' existences are separate from the human mind and human thoughts (the opposite of **subjectivism**). For example, saying, "Ice cream is delicious" is subjective, whereas stating, "the ice cream has chocolate chips" is objective. The latter statement is true by itself because it is not affected by individual opinion.

Postmodernism: The anti-movement to modernism, it literally means "after modernism." Enlightenment modernism was a major philosophy in 18th century Europe that supported the dismissal of tradition in favor of rationalism, skepticism, and empiricism. Postmodernism, by contrast, asserts that there is no way to discover objective Truth.

Rationalism: The philosophy that reason alone, or ***a priori***, knowledge is requisite for belief (the opposite of **empiricism**).

Skepticism: A philosophical approach to truth based on the necessity to question and doubt knowledge, including religious truth claims.

Socratic Method: The technique of interrogation used by Socrates to demonstrate inconsistent logic. Its purpose is to uncover contradictions in a person's beliefs so that he or she will then establish more reliable convictions.

Subjectivism: The assertion that what may appear to be an objective truth, or a fact independent of the human mind, is merely a disguised opinion, for the mental state of the person speaking colors the truth of a statement (the opposite of **objectivism**). The declaration, "This music is loud," for example, might seem to be an objective fact, but it really means, "*I* think that this music is loud." Such opinions vary from person to person and thus cannot be objective truths.

Theism: The belief in a personal God who interacts with the world and with humans (the opposite of **atheism**).

---

*I am indebted to Emily Serrell, who composed this glossary after carefully researching several standard philosophy reference works.

BIBLIOGRAPHY

Allen, Woody. *Getting Even.* New York: Random, 1971.

__________. *Side Effects.* New York Random, 1980.

__________. *Without Feathers.* New York Random, 1975.

Barth, Karl. *The Humanity of God.* Atlanta: John Knox, 1960.

Bjorkman, Stig. *Woody Allen on Woody Allen: In Conversation with Stig Bjorkman.* New York: Grove, 1993.

De Vries, Peter. *The Blood of the Lamb.* New York: Signet, 1961.

____________. *The Mackerel Plaza.* New York: Signet, 1958.

Downey, Michael. *Altogether Gift: A Trinitarian Spirituality.* Maryknoll, NY: Orbis, 2000.

Edgerton, Clyde. *Killer Diller.* New York: Ballantine, 1991.

Eichhoefer, Gerald W., ed. *Enduring Issues in Philosophy.* San Diego: Greenhaven, 1995.

Einstein, Albert. *Ideas and Opinions.* New York: Dell, 1954.

Ellul, Jacques. *Reason for Being: A Meditation on Ecclesiastes.* Trans. J. Hanks. Grand Rapids: Michigan, 1990.

Grenz, Stanley J. *A Primer on Postmodernism.* Grand Rapids: Eerdmans, 1996.

Hart, Trevor. *Faith Thinking: The Dynamics of Christian Theology.* Downers Grove: InterVarsity, 1995.

Henderson, Charles P. *God and Science: The Death and Rebirth of Theism.* Atlanta: John Knox, 1986.

Hick, John & Brian Hebblethwaite. *Christianity and Other Religions.* Philadelphia: Fortress, 1980.

Kreeft, Peter, ed. *The Shadowlands of C. S. Lewis: The Man Behind The Movie.* San Francisco: Ignatius, 1994.

Lawson, Lewis A. & V. A. Kramer, eds. *Conversations with Walker Percy.* Jackson: Univ. Press of Miss., 1985.

______________________. *More Conversations with Walker Percy.* Jackson: Univ. Press of Miss., 1993.

Lewis, C. S. *A Grief Observed.* New York: Bantam: 1961.

________. *The Problem of Pain.* New York: Macmillan, 1962.

MacIntyre, Alasdair. *Whose Justice? Which Rationality?* Notre Dame: Univ. of Notre Dame Press, 1988.

MacLeish, Archibald. *J.B.* Boston: Houghton Mifflin, 1958.

________________. *Letters of Archibald MacLeish.* Ed. R. H. Winnick. Boston: Houghton Mifflin, 1983.

Magill, Frank N., ed. *Masterpieces of American Literature.* New York: HarperCollins, 1993.

Newbigin, Lesslie. *The Gospel in a Pluralist Society.* Grand Rapids: Eerdmans, 1989.

O'Connor, Flannery. *Mystery and Manners: Occasional Prose.* Ed. S. & R. Fitzgerald. New York: Noonday, 1969.

Okholm, Dennis L. & Timothy R. Phillips, eds. *Four Views On Salvation in A Pluralistic World.* Grand Rapids: Zondervan, 1996.

Percy, Walker. *The Moviegoer.* New York, Ivy: 1961.

Plath, James, ed. *Conversations with John Updike.* Jackson: Univ. Press of Miss., 1994.

Polanyi, Michael. *Knowing and Being.* Ed. Marjorie Grene. Chicago: Univ. of Chicago Press, 1969.

_________. *Personal Knowledge: Towards a Post-Critical Philosophy.* Chicago: Univ. of Chicago Press, 1962.

Speidell, Todd H. "Baseball, Dogmatism, and Relativism," *The Chaplain's Craft.* VI.1 (Fall 1993): 1-3.

_______________. "God, Woody Allen, and Job," *Christian Scholar's Review.* XXIX.3 (Spring 2000).

Tilley, Terrence W. *The Evils of Theodicy.* Eugene, OR: Wipf and Stock, 2000.

Torrance, T. F. *The Ground and Grammar of Theology.* Charlottesville: Univ. Press of Virginia, 1980.

_______________. *Transformation and Convergence in the Frame of Knowledge: Explorations in the Interrelations of Scientific and Theological Enterprise.* Grand Rapids: Eerdmans, 1984.

Tracy, David. *The Analogical Imagination: Christian Theology and the Culture of Pluralism.* New York: Crossroad, 1981.

Updike, John. *Hugging the Shore: Essays and Criticisms by John Updike.* New York: Vintage, 1983.

_________. *In the Beauty of the Lilies.* New York: Knopf, 1996.

__________. *Roger's Version.* New York: Ballantine, 1986.

Wiesel, Elie. *Messengers of God: Biblical Portraits and Legends.* Trans. Marion Wiesel. New York: Summit, 1976.

Wood, Ralph C. *The Comedy of Redemption: Christian Faith and Comic Vision in Four American Novelists.* Notre Dame: Univ. of Notre Dame, 1988.

Woodhouse, H. F. "The Limits of Pluralism." *Scottish Journal of Theology.* 34 (1981):1-15.

APPENDIX I

Miracle

The door was a dark mahogany, polished to such an unnatural sheen that I was prompted to check my teeth in its glow before I knocked. My knuckles hit its smooth surface twice, then descended. The brass nameplate was obvious on the door, its neat business lettering stark and precise.

James Q. Antagonist, Attorney-At-Law

Specializing in Moral and Spiritual Litigation
For over Three Hundred Years

No soul too small, No sin too large,
And always a fair price.

A pleasant-looking middle-aged woman answered the door, her dark hair pulled up in a severe bun, her navy business suit and skirt accented by tasteful, small pearl earrings and a strand of pearls close around her neck. “Hello,” she said, her voice pleasantly neutral. “Please have a seat in the waiting room. Mr. Antagonist will be with you shortly.”

I swallowed and nodded my thanks to her as she held open the door to allow me in. The air inside the waiting room was cool and dry. The room itself was rather bare, the chairs slightly uncomfortable, the walls a pale taupe color, decorated with inoffensive, guileless still-lives of flowers and fruit. I flipped through the customary pile of magazines on the end table: *The Afterlife Today*; *Karma 2000: New Reincarnations for a Newer You*, and *Elysian Digest*. I had barely cracked the cover of *The Afterlife Today* before I heard the same mildly toneless intrusion as before: "Mr. Antagonist will see you now."

I stepped into the office, my breathing quickening with apprehension. The lawyer was dark-haired and of medium height, with a pleasant, if somewhat insincere, smile. "Please have a seat."

He leaned back in his chair, sighing a little, and produced a scroll of thick white parchment from a desk drawer. He unrolled it and began to read, muttering softly to himself.

"My, my," said Antagonist.

I tightened my fingers on the armrests of the chair.

"Goodness gracious," he commented.

I liberated the right chair-arm from its death grip and began to gnaw voraciously at my right fingernails.

"Hmmm . . ." he ruminated.

I gave a small whimper as my teeth hit the quick of my index finger and began to rock back and forth in the chair.

"I see," he commented.

I restrained myself from assuming the fetal position. "Well?" asked a strangled, small voice I barely recognized as my own.

"Let's see here," he said, spreading the parchment out on the desk. "My, my. This *is* unusual. I haven't seen a case like this in years."

"And . . ."

"Well, I don't think there's anything I can do to help you."

"What do you mean, nothing you can do to help me?"

He tapped the parchment spread out on his desk. "You," he said, gesturing at me, "are a Miracle."

"What?" I said blankly.

"You," he continued, "are a Miracle. Your birth, originally unlicensed, was allowed only by special dispensation. Divine Intervention, if you will."

"What?"

He sighed. "I suppose you weren't made aware of this when you arrived."

I checked myself before I could say "what" again. "No. No I wasn't."

He sighed again, muttering something about bureaucracy, and pointed to a section that had apparently been copied onto the parchment. It appeared to be a standard government-style form, each blank filled in with neat, beautifully flowing golden script. I recognized my own name, those of my parents, and my birth date.

"You see," he proceeded, cool and businesslike, "you were not originally supposed to have existed at all. You were slated to die here—" he gestured to a spot on the form, a date two days after my birth, with a line neatly drawn through it. "However, due to unique extenuating circumstances, your termination was, well . . . terminated. In layman's terms, a Miracle."

"Oh," I said faintly.

"Now . . . According to Dispensatory Trial Edict 4007653-A, no Person of Miraculous Origin shall undergo Spiritual Judgment in a Court of Law."

"Well, then, what happens to the charges? Are they dropped?"

His facial expression changed from dull to serious. "Oh, my word, no. Charges like these require a special probative hearing."

"Couldn't you represent me before the probate judge?"

His look was almost one of pity. "Oh, no. There is no probate judge. Under Article 760812 of the Standard Revised Judgmental System, all Miracles facing charges after Death must, in the presence of jurors, face their own conscience."

I figured if I fidgeted any harder, my thumbs would fly off and go spiraling through the air. Just when I had decided to turn and walk off down the hall and forget the whole thing entirely to try and get through the afterlife without it, a figure opened the heavily paneled door, gesturing inward. "This way, please." The voice was quiet but commanding. Numb, I followed.

The room was still, silent, and dim. A pale, vague light filled it, as though from above, but I could not see fixtures or distinguish walls. The light merely faded slowly into an inky, impenetrable blue-blackness.

Directly before me in the dim light was a marble stool standing in a small, empty place. Timidly, I made my way to it.

The man who had beckoned me in now stood directly before me, smiling slightly. "Case number 42309f?"

"Um, yes."

"What shall I call you?"

I gulped. "Um, you can call me Al."

His smile broadened almost imperceptibly. "Hello, Al. I'm . . ."

"Wait," I said before I could even realize that I probably shouldn't interrupt. "I mean, uh, your Honor, aren't you, um . . ."

"Plato?"

"Um, yes," I said, noting his broad shoulders and the expression of quiet wisdom in his eyes.

"You don't have to call me your Honor," he said gently. "This isn't a trial, remember?"

"Then what is it?" I asked apprehensively.

"It's a chance to evaluate the opportunities you were given in life—the ones you took and the ones you gave up. As a Miracle, we took a chance on your even being born. I'm here to help you make sure that you made the most of your life."

"But . . . Why now? I'm not alive. There's not anything I can do about it now!"

His expression turned reproving. "Perhaps you should have thought about that earlier."

"Are you saying that I wasted my life?" I asked, thunderstruck.

"I'm here to help you figure that out—to straighten out the events of your past life before you move on to the next, to correct any misconceptions you might have had about the way the world works—or at least about the way it worked, this time around."

"So I'm guessing there is a God," I said stiffly.

"God? You mean a Supreme, All-powerful Being? The Alpha and Omega? The Eternal One?"

"Yes, that's what I mean."

"Yes."

Oh, great, I thought. *I pissed Him off.* "Uh . . . Is He angry with me?"

"No. Not really."

"What?" I murmured. *His eye is on the sparrow, and I know he watcheth me.* "Does he have *better* things on his mind?"

"Don't be unreasonable," he objected quietly. "Let's let things come as they will, shall wc?"

"All right," I acquiesced ungracefully.

"Now," continued Plato. "The charge against you is one of irreverent indifference. Do you understand what that means?"

I straightened out a little on my stool, indignant, and then realized that the philosopher had a point. "I know what the words mean," I confessed, "but in this context . . ."

"Well, Al, let me see if I can explain," he suggested, sitting down beside me on the cool marble. "Looking at your life, no one could say that you did not live it to the fullest. You contributed both to yourself and to the rest of mankind—perhaps not through direct charity for charity's sake, but rather through everyday thoughtfulness, frank friendliness, good humor, and levelheaded advice, because of your belief that doing good would cause others to repay your kindness. You experienced many wonderful and terrible things. You lived your life in accordance with your own ideas and made a unique place for yourself in the world. Yours was a very bold existence by any standard, most especially so for a person who described herself as cowardly.

"There are, however, certain things in your life that you did neglect. Although a very intelligent person, you had, and still do have, a rather alarming tendency to ignore life's fundamental questions.

"You see, Al, you were gifted not only with miraculous life but also with unusual talent and superb intellect. You have a capacity for deep thought, a gift well-suited to probing the mystery of human life and existence, but you often ignored such questions.

"Afraid of what you might uncover and more secure in doubt than in the quest for a truth you might not be prepared to accept, you would calmly and neatly debate the particulars of life, and even of God on occasion. You never reached any conclusion or conviction to live by. Whenever the discussion turned serious, you would confess you were 'still seeking,' even though the fact of the matter was you had never begun the search.

"You were always comfortable thumbing your nose at the Almighty, whose existence you did not acknowledge or even contemplate to the best of your abilities. Your life was well-planned and successful, but as for the rest . . ."

"Yes," I replied softly. "I see."

"So that's why you're here," he continued.

"Oh." There was a deep, sudden silence I hurried to fill. "Then what are you doing here?"

"I'm here to help you," Plato answered me simply.

"Oh," I said again.

The silence crept in again, stealthily, almost before I knew it. "Why?" I whispered.

"That is what you are here to find out," he replied.

"Do you mind if I get some reference material?" I timidly asked.

He smiled. "I think I have just the thing." He retreated into the deep blue-blackness and returned with a home movie projector. He set it on the cool marble floor, tinkering with it until it threw a square of grainy whitish-yellow light up against the inky, mysterious darkness that surrounded us. He gave it a few good kicks, and a picture formed, fuzzed, and finally focused. I recognized the scene as I would one from a dream.

"Chapter one," he said coolly. "You were born."

As I watched highlights of my life flashing before my eyes, I realized that Plato was right. Although I had done a lot of deep thinking in my time, I had never really found where I stood with respect to life's fundamental questions. Yet somehow as I watched myself in that grainy square of light, I realized that I had known all along; I just hadn't let myself know. Slowly the film ground to a stop. The picture skipped and then ceased altogether, leaving us alone again in the dimness. I felt a sudden pang of longing for the people and places of my former life.

Plato flipped a switch on the projector and the light faded out of existence, leaving us totally alone in the dimness. The air seemed to weigh heavily in on me.

"What do you think?" he prompted me.

"I'm not s . . ." I stopped myself. The answer was so familiar; so comfortable; so safe, it had become automatic. "I think I understand."

"Tell me what you've learned."

I smiled a little at myself, and suddenly realized that it was the first time I had smiled in days. "My life wasn't meaningless."

"Yes?"

"It had plenty of meaning," I said slowly. "Just none that I was able to see." I paused, correcting myself. "None that I was willing to see."

"Yes?"

"I laughed at the absurdity of God and of life, when I didn't even realize that it was humanity I was mocking. Myself, not God. My interpretation of the Infinite, the Unknowable. It was what I made it, and I made it laughable."

The silence settled in briefly before I resumed. "But that doesn't mean that it wasn't real." It returned, and I realized that the heaviness in the air was the weight of my own discovery.

"I prevented myself from learning the truth about life, about God, about everything. Because I was afraid—afraid of looking stupid, afraid of being wrong. Afraid of failing where it counted the most. I wanted to be sure . . . and the fact is. . . Well, the fact was that you can't be certain. Not now . . . I mean, not then. There's no way. That's no way to live your life: as I did, fearing Hell and dreaming Heaven and hoping that Purgatory was a reasonable compromise; committing to neither in case Mohammed was right after all. Life, learning, understanding—it's not like that. It's not about being afraid.

"I knew all along what I believed to be true: not duality or plurality but reality. I knew the truth. Yes, yes, I think I *did* know the truth. But I was afraid. Afraid that it was a lie, afraid that it was fiction. I feared the terrible power that that meant I must have—the power not only to create and to live within my own universe, but also to, through my actions, ensure my place in a larger cosmos that operated completely independently of me. And, most frightening of all, to realize that Truth, that Universal Truth, that Eternal Light was outside me—outside me in that I could not dictate its truth nor change it solely by the force of my mind, but also *inside* me too—inside me in that truth and mystery were right there for the taking all the time. That understanding was never out of reach, but it is only now, now that I can't fear losing my self—losing my soul—that I can apprehend."

I recovered and looked around me, suddenly tired, as if I had just finished weeping. The room was suddenly warm. Growing within me I felt a soft, safe, soothing comfort, an inimitable, quiet elation, somehow like the feeling I felt as a child, safe in my father's arms.

A single ray of light penetrated the dimness, stretching, glowing, growing, filling the room as the darkness retreated before it until the whole room was visible, a fantastic structure of silver and alabaster and marble, as warm as the summer sun. The stone itself seemed soft and inviting. I looked for my guide, but he was gone. The light surrounded and enveloped me, warming and caressing me with the kiss of a light breeze. My body became kindling for the fire of this childish delight, this wondrous discovery, this safety, this joy.

"Is it like this for everyone?" I whispered.

And suddenly, I knew.

The Search

Why are we here? What is our purpose in life? Why must life be so difficult for some and so easy for others? These are all questions that have plagued humanity throughout history. Man has always striven to understand his reason for being alive. He does this because he cannot understand why God would put him on a planet for no apparent reason. So is the case with Mike Larkin, who struggles with the meaning and sometimes the meaninglessness of life.

"Beep-beep, beep-beep," Mike's alarm clock flashed 6:20, and it was time for him to go to work at his job at Chemtec, a biotechnology company at which he was the software specialist. As he got out of bed and went to brush his teeth, he thought to himself sarcastically, "Another day at the mill. I wonder if anything exciting will happen today?" Mike's wife, Michelle, woke up around the same time he did, so luckily he had a companion with whom he could converse. "Honey, do you think I am a happy man?" he asked her.

She responded, "Well, dear, you really haven't been yourself lately—or even for the past couple of weeks."

"That's funny," Mike replied. "That's about the same time that I realized that this job is really taking me nowhere. I mean, my boss is a huge jackass. If a position is open, I won't get it because he doesn't feel that I'm competent enough to be promoted. And there is no possible way that I can get a raise. I just feel like I am driving on a street that eventually is going to dead end."

Mike and his wife continued to converse about her job and the kids, and then he went down to eat breakfast and leave. During his 45-minute commute that should have taken fifteen minutes, he thought more about how his job was a dead end. Then he delved more deeply into his feelings. "How did I come to have this job?" he wondered. "Do I have any impact on the world at all by having this job? If I am on this earth, surely God wants me to do something meaningful with my life." But he soon pushed these thoughts to the back of his head and continued his commute to work.

After he was done with work, Mike went down to a local bar to eat some wings and have a few drinks. There he met up with some of his old high school friends whom he had not seen in a while. They did the usual catching up on each other's lives and reminiscing over old times, but then they got on the subject of their jobs. Mike groaned when he heard about how everybody else had their dream job and how their lives could not get any better. Then Mike told them about his situation, at which point his friend Joe said, "Hey, Mike, do you remember John, the really rowdy kid who always got in trouble?"

Mike nodded in agreement.

"Well, do you know what happened to him? He became a priest!"

"You're kidding!" Mike exclaimed.

"Nope," stated Joe. "He's going to be in town tomorrow, if anybody's interested in seeing him."

Mike then thought to himself, "Hmm . . . maybe I should see him some time this week. I think he can help me with my problem at work."

The friends' dinner meeting then adjourned and Mike drove home. As he was pulling up to his house he saw that paint was flaking off and that the roof did not look in such good shape, either. He thought, "Jeez, I've really let this house slip lately, but I don't make enough money to fix anything, so hopefully we can live with this until winter."

Mike went inside, said "Hi," and "Good night," to his kids and went upstairs to go to bed. After he performed his nightly ritual of brushing his teeth and washing his face, he headed into bed. But as he saw his seldom-used Bible lying on his nightstand, he thought to himself that he might leaf through it just a little bit. Before he could, however, his wife came up.

"Honey," announced Michelle, "I was just thinking that I am really happy here, and so are the kids. I feel that God has blessed us by putting us here in Minnesota."

"Well, I'm glad you feel that way, dear," muttered Mike.

"Why do you say that, Mike?" questioned Michelle.

"I mean that I agree with you that God has blessed us with our location. I mean, there is a low crime rate, the schools are great, and we are surrounded by beautiful lakes, but I feel that I am paying for all of this goodness by having a meaningless job. I look at our house with the leaky roof and our flaking paint, and then I see people driving these nice cars on their way to their plush homes, and they always have smiles on their faces. Do they *ever* feel bad? Sometimes I don't understand how life can be so good to some people and so bad to others."

"Well, Mike, if your job is getting to you *that* much, then maybe you should look for some other place of employment. Anyway, you're going fishing this weekend with your old high school buddies, aren't you? That should relieve some stress."

"Oh, yeah, I forgot about that. Sometimes I feel that the only place where I can be alone with my thoughts and feelings is out there on the lake in our little boat," sighed Mike. With that, they went to sleep.

The next morning Mike got up and repeated his morning routine. Then he drudged through his workday, all the while looking forward to Saturday and his fishing trip with his friends. The day ended and at last he was ready to head home, but then he remembered that his friend John was in town.

"The only problem," Mike thought, "is that I don't know where he is staying." Luckily, last night Joe had given Mike his number, so Mike quickly called him up and found out John's hotel and room number.

As he went up the elevator, he thought, "What am I doing? John doesn't want to be bothered with my problems; people probably come to him all the time with their problems and I bet he gets fed up with it." At that point he was about to turn back, but reason prevailed and he decided to go through with it. He arrived at John's room and knocked on the door; a pleasant voice answered, "Come in."

Mike entered the room and they exchanged greetings and caught up on old times as usual, but then they got down to business. Mike told John about his situation at work and how it was affecting his life. He also told him about his views on life, how sometimes he felt it could be meaningless and unfair. John responded, "Mike, I have some good news for you. You are not the first person to ask these questions, nor will you be the last. There is also an answer to these questions."

"Really!?" Mike exclaimed.

"Yes, really, Mike. The answers are all found here in the Good Book," said John as he patted his Bible. "You see, there is a book in here called Ecclesiastes that deals with these exact questions. King Solomon wrote it in 935 BC, and he experienced the same things you are experiencing. He starts right off by saying that 'everything is meaningless,' that 'there is nothing new under the sun,' and that all that we do in life is 'a chasing after the wind'" (1:2, 9, 14).

If you pursue material possessions and wealth as your only goals, you will never be satisfied, because satisfaction is one of God's gifts to us (5:19). But if you have God in your heart and pursue these things in moderation, you will become satisfied. Basically, "Fear God and keep his commandments, for this is the whole duty of man" (12:13).

So you shouldn't be jealous of those rich people, because they are going to die someday just like you will (2:16). But as for your work, my advice to you is to find something that you love to do and make that your occupation. We don't know how long we are going to be on this earth, so we might as well find something that makes us happy and do that for the rest of our lives" (9:2ff).

Mike responded, "Wow. I don't know how I can thank you; you have given me new perspective on my life." Mike went home, contemplated his life, and joined the Lutheran Church.

When he was on a fishing trip the next weekend, it dawned on him, "That's it. I have every record for every type of fish on all of the lakes in a fifty-mile radius around here. I could open up my own guide service and take people to the best spots." Mike was an excellent fisherman, and he seemed to have a knack for finding the trophy fish. The next year, he and his family opened up a guide business on a local lake that soon got a reputation for finding the best fish. Eventually, the Larkins got too old to take care of it anymore and moved into a nursing home. Their nurses say that when they died, they both had smiles on their faces.

APPENDIX II

Is Faith Compatible with Science?

Sam and I were both surprised when we found out that we had to write a biology essay last period on Thursday afternoon. When we walked into the quiet room and saw "Where did Man come from?" written on the board and fourteen other students scribbling on sheets of paper stacked on their desks, our hearts sank. Sam was more upset than I was—I actually knew something about evolution and Darwin's theory of natural selection, so I was able to wing the essay pretty easily. The next day when our teacher handed the essays back, mine read, "Good Job. A-." I turned around to ask Sam how he did and was shocked to see him near tears, holding his single sheet of paper. A large red "F" was at the top. Sam hadn't wasted any words; in fact, I was able to read his entire essay before he got a chance to say anything:

> God created Man. The Bible tells us that God took six days to create the universe and rested on the seventh. The first people were Adam and Eve. They ate the apple from the forbidden tree, so they were expelled from the Garden of Eden. Then they proceeded to have children. We are their descendants.

At the bottom, also in red, the teacher had written: "Is this a joke?"

"Okay, I give up. What was the right answer?"

I couldn't believe that Sam had actually written something he learned in our Sunday school class. Hadn't he even heard of Darwin? "Sam, evolution," I told him. "Billions of years of natural selection . . ." I did not understand how this was news to him; we had been studying this for the past week in biology.

After class he just walked off, pretty shaken after having failed the essay.

I didn't see Sam again until Sunday morning after church when we were both waiting for the bell to ring for Sunday school. He seemed much happier now; the first thing he said to me was, "Wow, I understand it now. I read all about Darwin yesterday."

"That's great. Hope you do better on the test."

"Oh, I will."

Sunday school was something I never found very interesting. Unlike most of my friends' Sunday school classes, where all the kids sat around and talked about life and what the Christian thing to do was, we got lectured by a priest. Father Donovan taught at the local Catholic school, and on Sundays he came to our church to instruct us in the ways of God and our Savior Jesus Christ.

Sam and I sat in the back again this week and tried not to pay attention to the lesson. We had done this all throughout Sunday school, because usually the teacher was a volunteer from the community who could not control the rowdier kids. Amid the paper throwing and other distractions, goofing off had always been pretty easy. This year, though, since they brought in Father Donovan, three students had already been expelled. Though most of us would consider not having to attend Sunday school any more a blessing, the parents of Larry, Chris, and Tom were so scandalized by their children's behavior that they sent them to Catholic school to be straightened out. We hadn't seen or heard from them since.

So when we heard Father Donovan call out Sam's name, we both froze.

"Yes, Father Donovan?"

"What do you think?"

"About what, sir?"

"About Genesis." Pause. "Would you give us a summary of where we come from, Samuel?"

After a short pause, I winced as I saw Sam's face brighten up; I knew he was relieved because he thought that he knew this one. "Well, Father," he began, "Billions of years of natural selection have produced highly evolved species like ourselves. According to Charles Darwin . . ." I really expected Father Donovan to let him have it, so I quickly poked Sam and shook my head subtly.

Instead of lecturing Sam, Father Donovan looked strangely at us and started laughing. Then he asked me, "What do you think?"

"Father, sir . . ." I quickly scrambled for an answer. "God created man. The first people were Adam and Eve."

The priest continued to laugh, and I was confused. "Well, you are both correct," Father Donovan answered.

"What?" I asked.

"Evolution is a fact—the church has accepted this, but it need not be contrary to the basic foundation of our faith, that God created us.

Evolution is . . ." he paused. "Evolution is God's tool. Do you understand?"

"Yeah, I guess," I responded. I guess I really did. I do not think that Sam did, though.

"Okay, good," said Father Donovan, and he continued his lecture.

The next day at school, I knew for sure that Sam did not get it. He was asking Mr. Robertson, our biology teacher, about evolution and God.

"You see, Sam, everybody knows that science is right. You can't really deny it. So the church, over the years, has contested various scientific facts and eventually admitted that they were wrong and joined the rest of the world."

"Like a flat Earth."

"Exactly. And the sun revolves around the Earth, right? Anyway, so eventually the Catholic Church realized that it needed to catch up with the educated world and said, 'Hey, yeah, I guess we were wrong, but we weren't *that* wrong . . . ,' and they tried to reconcile it with their old faith and make everything better."

"Wait, so you don't think you can combine the two?"

"Just look at the Bible. There is a very specific order laid out for how God created Earth. For example, according to Genesis, God created the universe. Then he created light, and then he created the sky. After the sky, he made vegetation. *Then* he created the sun, the moon and the stars. After that, he made fish and other sea creatures, birds, wild animals and livestock. Finally, he created man."

"So?"

"Well, if you've been keeping up with your reading, or if you'd just think about it, you'd realize that that's not the way things happened. They couldn't have. The order in which the scientific community has come to accept is very different from the creationist account. What about dinosaurs, for example? Not to mention countless other scientifically impossible stories in the Bible."

"Okay, okay . . . Well, Fr. Donovan said we shouldn't take those stories literally. They focus on God as the Creator and on his special relationship to humanity."

"Since when could you pick and choose what is actually true in the Bible? It sounds to me like more trouble than it's worth to constantly be trying to reconcile this obviously antiquated mythology with mainstream science."

"Okay . . ."

"I mean, as science expands and explains more and more things, there is less and less room for a worldview that contains a God. What does God do all day? It appears that he does nothing and never did. Some God."

Sam did not know what to believe; to be honest, neither did I. We talked about it a few times after those weird few days happened, but we both decided that it was confusing and never really came to a firm conclusion.

"I just can't sort it all out. I mean, I can believe evolution; I can believe in God, but what's the point? Mr. Robertson was telling me about Occam's razor. We don't really need God to explain life on earth, so why do we bother? But then again, I don't want to just dismiss God like that. I've been brought up my whole life to believe in Him."

"Yeah, I don't know." I guess I didn't.

Discussion questions:

- Is Mr. Robertson's rejection of creationism scientific shrewdness or a statement of his own faith in atheism?

- Given the different modes of thinking involved in each, is a compromise of science and religion valid?

APPENDIX III

The Case of Alan

Alan decided to eat at his favorite restaurant, Roman's Pizzeria, as he considered the meaning of tragic events in his recent life. As luck would have it, his two best friends, Shawn and Alex, had already ordered a large pepperoni pie with extra sauce and fresh garlic. Their spicy meal matched their pungent debate, a topic they had often revisited. Shawn defended God's nature as all-good and all-powerful, and Alex questioned how such a God could permit evil. Their contention had both interested and amused Alan in the past, but on this Saturday evening Alan's heart-rending circumstances of late focused their somewhat academic discussion onto his personal crisis.

Alan unburdened his heart as his two friends empathetically listened. "My father's problems stemmed from his humble beginnings," Alan began his story. "His family struggled to provide food, clothing, and the bare necessities of life for him and his five siblings. When he became older, he pursued a career in business to ensure that he would always have enough to provide for him and his family. He seemed to feel that material success would compensate for the feeling of impoverishment and inadequacy that were his burden to bear."

"How did that affect your family?" Shawn probed.

"My parents wanted me to be successful," Alan replied, "even at an early age. I was introverted, reflective, creative, and imaginative; they wanted me to be outgoing and athletic. I realize now why I felt inadequate as a kid: their expectations for me squelched my natural proclivities, and so I lost self-confidence."

"Were they obsessed with money?" queried Alex.

"Definitely," Alan emphatically agreed. "They pitied the poor, and prided themselves in new cars, bigger houses, and nicer possessions. They also pressured me to live up to their standards. At school, I pitied geeks and dorks, and I felt good about myself when I joined the popular crowd. My parents 'successfully' molded me to fit their ideals of an acceptable child.

"When I became a Christian in middle school, I was too zealous for their comfortable style of Christianity, and they asked me to tone down my fanaticism. And kids at school poked fun at me for being a 'preacher.' I was ashamed that I cared more about the adoration of others than the service of God, but fitting in was very important to me. I felt inadequate when I displeased my parents and my friends, but when I pleased them, I felt inadequate again for disappointing God."

"Just like your dad felt inadequate," Shawn observed.

"Yes," Alan agreed. "He was driven by a deep need for approval, and I now realize that I felt the same way. So I experimented with drugs in high school and adopted a fashionable skepticism toward religious belief. But when I attended a Young Life retreat, it was fun, active, and social—just as my parents wanted—and it was a genuine spiritual experience for me.

“Back on track with God, I began theological study in a high school course and even attended an optional theological discussion group that met during lunch time. My parents again became concerned that such reflective activity would derail me from Student Government, sports, and other ‘fast track’ activities.

“And then my dad fell off his ‘fast track.’ I’ll never forget that day. The principal called me into his office, and his anguished face conveyed a sense of tragedy. My father’s compulsion to succeed had propelled him into a fantastic scheme of financial improprieties. He swindled clients, relatives, and friends. And when his scam collapsed, his shame surfaced. He could endure it no longer, and he took his own life.”

Alan intensely looked at both friends as he angrily confessed with tears in his eyes, “My question earlier on in my life was, ‘Am I good enough for God?’ but now I really want to know, ‘Is God good enough for me?’”

When he finished unburdening himself to his two friends, they sat in silence for a few minutes, affixing their eyes on his sullen face. They took a brief break to order another pizza and to ponder the impact of this tragedy upon Alan’s life. Both invited him to their regular place of fellowship and discussion: Shawn suggesting he visit the Church of the Good Samaritan and Alex encouraging him to visit the East Tennessee Rationalist Society. Alan felt torn between his two friends and his two different futures: reaffirming his faith in God or abandoning his faith in God in favor of a belief in human reason.

In the Eyes of the Portrait

The rain pounded loudly on the windowpane as the light flickered on the ceiling. Tom Dobson stared blankly at the blurry floor, a tear trickling down his face. Father Patrick Johnson just sat and observed the scene of a father pining over the loss of his only child, Caroline, due to a drunk driver.

After about ten minutes of silence, Tom glanced up from the floor, only to be confronted by Caroline's portrait hanging on the living room wall. He took in a deep breath and weakly uttered a trembling "Why?"

Realizing that Tom had now broken the ice of silence, Father Patrick made circles on the olive carpet with the toe of his shoe, searching for words. "Tom," he started, "God loves you. You must always remember that. He has a plan for you, as he does for all people. Caroline's death was not a waste, and although you may not be able to understand it now, God has the situation in His hands. I firmly believe that He is holding Caroline in His arms as we speak."

Staring in utter disbelief, Tom shifted positions in his red leather chair, attempting not to look at Caroline's picture, which stared at him with painful eyes. "Father, can you honestly tell me that *my* God, the God that I have loved with my whole heart all my life, would take my baby, the thing I love most of anything in this world, and then proclaim that it was an act that needed to happen; that served some kind of purpose?" Tom paused for a few seconds and tried to regain his composure. "What kind of God would take my baby girl away from me? What have I ever done to deserve this? There are murderers out there, and people who worship Satan, and they still have their daughters. I lead Sunday school classes! I have lived every day for the Lord since I was seven years old. Why is He doing this to me?"

Father Patrick looked compassionately at Tom. Deeply moved by the strong emotion Tom was displaying for his daughter, Father Patrick himself was on the verge of tears. "The mysteries of the Lord are unfathomable; man can never understand them. He is almighty and powerful. The entire universe is . . ."

"You know what, Father?" Tom interrupted. "I don't believe that God is watching over me. I don't know if I even believe in God right now. I don't want to believe in a God that would do this to me. Caroline was a good girl who always lived her life to glorify God. She brought people closer to Christ daily, and she still had work to do. God can't be who I previously believed him to be . . . if he is anyone at all." Tom's face twisted with emotion. He rose and paced around the room, passing his hand over the mantelpiece. He still refused so much as a glance up the staring face of Caroline, the only witness to their conversation.

"Remember, Tom, the Lord also sacrificed His Son, so that all might live in the Kingdom of Heaven. Jesus was perfect, but God *allowed* Him to be slain. He could have stopped it, but he refused, so that you, I, Caroline, and all mankind may live with Him forever." Father Patrick watched as Tom began to relax and listen. "Why don't you sit back down, Tom?"

Returning to his leather chair, which still held the imprint of his body, Tom began to weep. With effort, he allowed a few words to escape: "He still took away my Caroline. She had so much life to live . . . she wasn't finished yet. Seventeen is too young to die . . . and did it have to be in a car wreck? She was in p-p-pain . . ." Tom's sentence broke off into stuttering and tears.

Glancing up at the portrait of Caroline on the wall, Father Patrick saw her familiar smile shine, radiant, upon her face. He thought about how beautiful she had been, both inside and out. She had truly been a child of Christ and had lived her life to the glory of His name. Tom Dobson's struggling word, "pain," was echoing through Father Patrick's mind. "Caroline is in Heaven right now," he said gently. "She can no longer sense any bit of pain. Aren't you happy for her because she no longer has to experience the torment of living on this earth? Instead, she is blessed with the eternal bliss of Heaven. She is completely at peace right now, and she has been able to touch the Almighty Father this very night. That is amazing to me. The Lord has blessed her with an early admittance into Heaven, which is the final goal of all mankind."

"Maybe, Father, but why is the Lord punishing me with this torment? Nothing is worse than losing a child."

"Don't think of it as punishment, Tom. This experience is only another of life's lessons. Think of Job, and of how he was tested. He lost everything he owned, and he lost all of his children, but he continued to stay faithful to the Lord, and he was richly blessed."

Tom finally allowed himself to look up at his daughter's picture. The light shone brightly off of the picture's mahogany frame. Caroline's sparkling blue eyes seemed to playfully tell him that everything was all right, and that she did not want him to hurt any more. "I still don't want to believe that my Lord would take my little girl. Is there any way that it could have just happened without his allowing it?"

Father Patrick toyed with the silver cross dangling from his neck. He drew a deep breath. "Yes. But doesn't that make you feel scared? In saying this, Tom, you're saying that the Lord does not have total control over all of the world. You're saying that events just *happen*, and that He turns his back."

Tom, beginning to lose control again, raised his voice in angry questions. "Then how else do you explain the Holocaust? What good came from that? How else do you explain the millions of little children starving in Africa? How else do you explain earthquakes and hurricanes? What good could possibly come from any of these things? If you don't mind my saying so, Father, I think your argument contains quite a few holes."

"The mysteries of the Lord are deep," Father Patrick calmly explained. "Who are we to even attempt to understand them?"

"Maybe," stated Tom as he stared into the storm outside. He could feel Caroline's eyes burning into him from the wall above. "All I know is, my faith has been taken to a place where I must question it in ways I've never questioned it before. I have to question my church. I have to question my life. I even have to question my God . . . that's all I know now."

Tom glanced about the room, looking for guidance. The bookshelf next to Tom's chair held many books that he had read in college. He saw a red hardback Dostoyevsky novel covered in a thick layer of dust and seized it in a desperate attempt to aid his argument. Turning to a heavily marked page in the book, he attempted to formulate his argument. "How do you argue against the great Dostoyevsky?" Tom stammered. "When it comes to God's permitting the death of innocent children, he says this: 'And if it is really true that [children] must share responsibility for all their father's crimes, such a truth is not of this world and is beyond my comprehension.' He goes on, 'It's not worth the tears of that one tortured child who beat itself on the breast with its unexpiated tears to "dear, kind God"! It's not worth it, because those tears are unatoned for. They must be atoned for, or there can be no harmony. But how? How are you going to atone for them? Is it possible?' "

"This is true," agreed Father Patrick. "But remember, the Lord still loves you. Although you have lost your child, try to keep in mind the things the Lord blesses you with every day. Caroline is still with you in spirit. She will be for the rest of your life. Just think about what you will be sacrificing by turning from God.

"The decision lies in your hands."

A Philosophical Journey with Lauryn Hill (Part One)

But way before my record deal,
The streets that nurtured Lauryn Hill
Made sure that I'd never go too far
Every ghetto, every city and suburban place I've been
Make me recall my days in the New Jerusalem

You know it's hot, don't forget what you've got

Looking back,
Looking back, looking back, looking back

It is a bright, warm day in South Orange, New Jersey. Reminiscing about her days as a young girl, Lauryn Hill sits in the park, watching people pass. She hears a young woman scolding her child. As Lauryn turns to see what is going on, she notices that the woman is only a teenager, yet she has a toddler-aged daughter. The little girl has dropped her ice cream cone on the sidewalk and her mother is scolding her. The strawberry ice cream slowly melts into the cracks in the concrete.

"You should know better! I just spent two dollars on that ice cream and you just wasted it! I ought to make you eat it off the ground!" the teenager nags. The girl begins to cry. "Shhhh . . . don't cry, okay? Mama's just a little bit low on cash right now and we don't have money to waste. Just be more careful, okay sweetheart?" The girl nods her head sheepishly.

Lauryn is curious. She has seen this picture many times before, but she wanted to know this woman's particular situation. Usually, she would dismiss the scene as just another teenage girl who did not act responsibly and now has been thrown full-force into motherhood. However, Lauryn suspects that something is different this time. As the family walks by, the young girl points and smiles at Lauryn.

"Don't point at people, Tyra. It's not polite. Wait a minute." The teenager grins and asks, "You're Lauryn Hill! I have your album and I listen to it with my daughter all the time. I love the way you mix R & B, hip-hop, reggae, and rap. You must be very proud of all the awards you've gotten."

Lauryn smiles weakly in return. "Yeah, the awards are great, but I'm worried that people have been ignoring my message. I didn't make those songs to make millions. I wanted to get my point across."

"Messages?"

"Of course! Those words came from my heart. If I have something to say, I'm gonna say it."

"So what do you have to say?"

"I thought you listened to my album all the time? Haven't you noticed my views? Haven't you paid attention to the messages about God and evil?"

"Well, I pay a lot of attention to the sound. That was what drew me to your music," explains the young woman. She sits down on the bench next to Lauryn, placing Tyra in her lap. "Besides, I've had some very stressful things happen to me in my short lifetime. Lately, I've been wondering where God is and what He's gonna do for me. You say that God is the only way to salvation, but how do I know He's gonna save me?"

"Ah, so you do listen to the words, don't you?" smirks Lauryn. "This is exactly why I wrote those songs. I know there are people just like you who need reassurance. God will see you through, but you've got to trust Him. So what has made you question God?"

"Let's see . . . My mother died of breast cancer when I was ten years old. My father has been taking care of my older brother and me by himself. He's always been strict. He expects only the best outta us. When I was fourteen, I was raped on the way home from basketball practice.

"I was afraid to tell my father about it. I was scared he'd get mad and blame me for it, or maybe even kick me outta the house. I decided instead to tell my brother, who was a junior in high school at the time. He's always been protective of me. All he wanted was revenge on the man who did this to me. Later, when I found out I was pregnant, I realized that I couldn't hide the secret from my dad any more. I told him about the rape and that I was pregnant. At first he didn't believe me. He said that I was just using rape as an excuse to cover up my irresponsibility. My brother tried to explain to Dad that it was the truth, but Dad can be pretty stubborn. I had to beg him not to kick me out.

"Finally, he decided to let me stay, but I had to raise the child on my own, support it on my own, and go to school. So, ever since Tyra was born, I've been working before and after school and putting her in day care while I'm in class. I'm only seventeen and I've been working like a thirty-year-old. My whole life has been determined by one incident. It's not like I deserved this. I haven't been sleeping around. Why has this happened to me?"

Lauryn begins to sing, "*I wrote these words for everyone/ Who struggles in their youth/ Who won't accept deception/ Instead of what is truth/ It seems we lose the game/ Before we even start to play/ Who made these rules?/ We're so confused/ Easily led astray/ Let me tell ya that/ Everything is everything/ Everything is everything/ After winter, must come spring/ Everything is everything.* See, that's exactly what has happened to you. All of these things have been happening to you and you don't know why. You're left searching for answers, and in the process, you've left God behind. What you need to do is *develop a negative into a positive picture.*"

"You mean 'look on the bright side'?" the girl asks.

"Exactly. For example, your little girl has changed your life dramatically. It may seem that her existence is bringing you down, but you need to think of little Tyra as a blessing, not as a curse. I'm sure there have been many times when she has brought joy into your life."

"Of course. I love Tyra with all my heart, but it's hard to forget all of the trouble I've been going through in order to support her."

"God has reasons for everything you are going through. We just don't know those reasons. And if we did know them, then what would be the point in God? We'd already know everything we want to know. You need to have faith in God and trust that he knows what he is doing. *Change comes eventually.* You'll get what's coming to you."

"But isn't it too late for me? I've already stated that I've doubted God. Hasn't He already turned His back on me?"

"*Now even when you're gone you can still be reborn/ And, from the night can arrive the sweet dawn.* It's never too late; you still have a chance. You just have to recognize God and believe that He will provide us with what we deserve."

"Well . . . All of this is starting to make sense. I guess I will start listening to your words more carefully, as well as the word of God. By the way, my name is Sheryl. It was very nice talking to you, Ms. Hill."

"Same to you, Sheryl. I hope I helped you out some. Just remember to look at the positive side of things. If you trust in God, then He will help you along the way. Accept Him into your life and He'll be there for you."

"Thanks. I'll make sure to remember that." Sheryl smiles as she leads Tyra down the sidewalk. The little girl waves to Lauryn as they pass, and then carefully avoids the deep cracks in the concrete. "*Step on a crack, break your mama's back.*"

A Philosophical Journey with Lauryn Hill (Part Two)

The unmerciful sun beats down on the concrete covered streets. It seems as if the rooftops will melt and slip off in black clumps to the boiling ground below. Lauryn Hill, however, is cool and calm in the recording booth. Her words are smooth and soothing, flowing easily into the microphone in front of her as she sings her songs from her heart, using her experiences as teaching tools for the "mis-educated."

After recording her songs, she steps out of the booth and smiles at the technician. "Hey, Richie. Keep cool."

"No kidding," he replies. "It's like the city is a huge oven."

She walks down the hallway until she reaches a lounge with black leather chairs on the sides, exotic plants in each corner, and African paintings on the walls. A small bar is on one side, and a coffee table is in the middle of the room. A young black man, decked out in Fubu gear and gold jewelry, reclines on one of the chairs. He jumps up as she passes him by.

"Yo, Lauryn Hill! Sup? I'm a big fan of yours and the Fugees. How you doin'?"

"Hi. Nice to meet you. And you are . . . ?"

"Meliek Williams. I go by 'Magnif.' That's short for 'magnificent.' You know—a stage name."

"Oh, I see. You're an artist. So, are you a rapper, a singer, or what?" she asks, ordering a bottle of water from the bar.

"Rapper all the way. Wanna hear some of my rhymes?"

"Sure," she agrees with a smirk. "Let's see what you've got."

Meliek starts rapping about life on the streets, gang violence, and drugs. At the same time, he glorifies it all. The blood, the corpses on the curbs, and the broken lives are all a bunch of fun and games that end with death.

Lauryn interrupts, holding up her hand. "Whoa! Whoa! Hold up! Is this what you're about? These are the ideas you want to send to people?"

The young man sinks back into his chair. "Why not? What's wrong with that? Everyone else is doing the same thing and making millions."

"So that's your excuse? Is that what you're going to say when five-year-old boys go around singing your lyrics—your words of hate, violence, and blood? I don't think so. You're gonna have to do better than that to get past 'Big L.'"

"Hey, sister, it's not my fault that little kids will listen to my music. That's what those little 'Parental Advisory' stickers are for. It's up to the parents to watch out for their kids."

"You're missing the point. Kids are looking for role models. Someone is going to look up to you and hang on every word you say. Do you want to influence a kid in that way?"

"I'm just looking for a living. I've gotta talent that I need to put to use."

"Well, I think you can put it to better use than what you've been using it for."

"But all kinds of rappers have been successful," he asserts as he stands back up.

"First off, your definition of 'success' isn't the same as mine. You're thinking of profit, as in money; I'm thinking of prophet, as in one who spreads God's Word."

"Aww . . . man! Don't start on that Gospel stuff. I've already been to church once this week!"

Lauryn takes a sip of water and swallows slowly before continuing her argument. "A church-going man, huh? That's hard to believe. How can you write such violent words and still accept God's Word? Going to church and then turning around and rapping about gats and gangs? *Gained the whole world for the price of your soul/ Tryin' to grab hold of what you can't control.*"

"Uhhh . . . my lyrics are just part of the business. You know, I'm just thinking of what will sell."

"Well, that brings me to my second point. Why be like everyone else? Why not stand out by making music that has a positive impact on people's lives? You need to find a wealth of wisdom before you think about an empire of gold. *Wisdom is better than silver and gold. Can't slick talk on the Day of Judgment.*"

Meliek sighs and stares at his feet.

"Your actions cause reactions. Don't think you won't face any consequences, because that's far from the truth. You got it all wrong. You *will* influence those kids. It might be a good influence; they might listen to your songs and decide that's not the type of life they want to live. More than likely, however, they are going to think your image of life is the way to live and it will be a bad influence on them. Things will come back to you. You will see the image that your lyrics have placed in children's eyes. Then you will realize that your 'gift' is being used for the wrong reasons. You need to listen to your heart."

"Okay! Okay! So I need to change my ways. But what am I supposed to rap about now? I'm not really sure what's in my heart. I've just been going by what people listen to."

"Well, I know for sure that you have something in your heart. What you have to do is block out what other people want you to do. Focus on what you want to do. You'll find what you're looking for. Just don't be seduced by the easy road."

"So this is what you did? You found success through saying what you believe in?"

"If you're talking money again, the answer is 'No.' I didn't look into my heart to find a way to make money. I looked into my heart to find truth, and the truth is in the Lord. He's my success."

"You make it sound so easy."

"I'm sorry to make it seem that way, because it's really not. If it were easy, then there would be less violent music and more music with spiritual meaning."

"All right. I guess I'll go home and try to listen to my heart. I have been headed in the wrong direction. But before I face the heat outside, do you want to hang out and lounge here for awhile and have a drink with me?"

"If you get too comfortable," Lauryn warns with a smile, "you might forget what we've talked about. *Now even when you're gone you can still be reborn/And from the night can arrive the sweet dawn.*"

The sun slowly sets over the hot city. Steam rises from the sidewalks as the cool moonlight crosses the corners. Finally, the sky turns blue, and it seems it may be as cool and calm outside as it is in the room.

APPENDIX IV

The Case of the Great Commission

"And he said unto them, Go into all the world and preach the gospel to every creature" (Mark 16:15).

Paige Patterson sat in his office one cold December afternoon, his head in his hands and his tie loosened. As the President of the sixteen-million-member Southern Baptist Convention, he was confused and upset about the imminent trip of thousands of missionaries to Chicago next summer. Normally, this would not be a problem; he could quietly recite Mark 16:15 (the Great Commission), and he would not feel the need for any other reassurance.

This time, however, the planned mission trip only provoked an angry response from the Council of Religious Leaders of Metropolitan Chicago: they insisted that sending his missionaries would only spark violence towards Jews, Hindus, Muslims, and Mormons in the city. How could the Council of Religious Leaders of Metropolitan Chicago tell him: "While we are confident that your volunteers would come with entirely peaceful intentions, a campaign of the nature and scope you envision could contribute to a climate conducive to hate crimes"?

"If they knew we are 'entirely peaceful,' then how could we possibly add to hate crimes?" he thought, remembering the letter he received telling him of mosques being vandalized in May and of six Orthodox

Jews being shot and wounded outside their synagogue in July. Although these events saddened him, it only convinced him more of the fact that people needed Jesus Christ in their lives! With Jesus Christ, they would find the love that they were looking for. And Christ *was* the only way: "I am the way, the truth, and the life. No man comes to the Father except through me" (John 14:6). As these issues flew in frenzy through Patterson's head, he heard a knock at the door.

Dr. Larry Gilmore, President of the Tennessee Baptist Convention, walked in with a distressed face. After clearing his throat, he addressed Patterson: "It seems," he said sorrowfully, "that the prayer booklets meant to educate Southern Baptists about those for whom they are to pray, Hindus, Jews, and Muslims, have fallen into the wrong hands." He looked mournfully at Patterson for some sign that he understood. When he stood up, Gilmore continued, "The passage about Hindus having 'darkness in their hearts that no lamp can dispel' has already prompted protests in India, Boston, and Houston."

"We were only trying to educate our fellow Christians about what they needed to focus on. Those books were never meant for distribution!"

"They weren't distributed, Paige! But somehow the religious groups have the books and they're upset, as they have a right to be. We cannot change it now, so what are we going to do?"

Just then Herb Hollinger, a spokesperson for the Southern Baptist Convention, stepped in. "Nothing!"

"What?" Patterson and Gilmore simultaneously responded, surprised by the new presence.

"Nothing," repeated Hollinger. "We don't have to do anything. Right now everyone in Chicago is up in arms because 100,000 missionaries are coming to teach the blessed love of Jesus Christ next summer. Anything we say or do right now will be criticized, as always!"

"We have been commissioned by God himself to teach everyone in every land about Him and His love," Gilmore answered. "'Therefore go and make disciples of all nations, baptizing them in the name of the Father and the Son and of the Holy Spirit, and teaching them to obey everything I have commanded you. And surely I am with you always, to the very end of the age' (Matthew 28:19-20)—these are the single most important verses in the planning of this trip. Paige, are you with us here?"

"Of course I know the Great Commission, Larry. Herb, I also know we are going to be picked on, no matter what we do. I refused the meeting with Gedale B. Horowitz (President of the New York-based Jewish Community Relations Council). I received a letter today that read, 'You have now made it crystal clear that your people cannot sit down with the very people who signed this letter of complaint and look them in the eyes and talk with them as friends. With regrets, I accept your refusal of our offer, and there the matter ends.'"

"So you refused the offer to meet with Horowitz and the six other Jewish leaders?" replied Herb, smirking.

"Yes, I did. I found that they were simply interested in the opportunity to bash Southern Baptists in the newspaper. I offered that I and seven other Southern Baptist leaders could meet Horowitz, six other Jewish leaders, and the top four administrators from Orthodox and non-Orthodox rabbinical schools. I had only two other conditions: one, that they understand that we will not abandon the proclamation of our faith, and two, that two of our eight will be 'Messianic Jews.' Then the International Fellowship of Christians and Jews said they would suspend relations with us until we stop 'targeting' them."

"I told the paper just today that Chicago will be the first stop in our 'Strategic Cities Initiative,' which is a plan to expand our Nashville-based church's southern stronghold," Herb replied. "I told them we might conduct a door-to-door campaign or hold neighborhood block parties. Then I tried to explain the booklet thing a little. Well, *that* went over like a lead balloon! I didn't touch on the letters, though, because I didn't know about them in detail yet."

Patterson turned and sat back down in his big comfortable chair; he was tired of talking and tired of thinking. He looked out his window and then picked up his Bible off the table to his left. He casually turned the pages to where he had turned so many times before and read the Great Commission aloud to Hollinger. He then placed his still-open Bible back on the table and closed his eyes. Gilmore and Hollinger stepped out of the room and disappeared down the hall, and again Patterson was left with the Gospel and the ever-present question, "Should we go?"

Hidden Beliefs

Daniel and Kathryn were driving home from the mall one day when Kathryn exclaimed, "Wow! Look at this beauty around us! God sure has made beautiful surroundings for us, don't ya think?"

Daniel smiled and simply nodded his head.

Kathryn again commented, "Well, I think that we should thank Him every day!"

After a while, Daniel replied, "Kate, I have to tell you something that you aren't going to like. I don't believe in God." Kathryn and Daniel had been dating for one and a half years; naturally, she was surprised. She thought back to all of the times that Daniel had gone to church with her and the one time when she had gone to church with him and his grandmother. She recalled all of the times that they had knelt together to give thanks to God, or to ask for guidance together. Tears suddenly welled up in her eyes.

"Kate, I'm sorry," said Daniel softly.

"Sorry? All those times we've been to church together, prayed together . . . you were leading me on! I used to talk to you about God and my beliefs and now I feel like an idiot because you probably never understood what I was talking about. I was looking to you for support. I should have known that something was up when you never really replied. I see it all clearly now." Kathryn burst into tears, her head in her hands.

Daniel pulled the truck into a local parking lot. "Nothing good has happened in my life for me to believe in. If there was a God, why would he have let my life be terrible all of those years?"

Kate looked up, replying, "God was watching over you all of those years. He protected you. Look where you are today. Don't you think that God has been gracious and good to you?"

"How can I believe that He has been gracious or good to me when I don't believe in God, Kate?" Daniel retorted, raising his voice.

"Just answer me this, then. All those times that we were praying together, who were you praying to?"

"Well, I wasn't exactly praying. I was wishing."

"Wishing?" Kathryn said as she let out an unbelieving laugh. "That is so wrong. You were lying to me."

"Listen, why do you care so much?"

"Well, aren't you afraid that you might go to hell? You should have told me!"

"God, there are so many 'could have's' and 'should have's,' but there is really nothing more that I can say. I believe what I believe, okay?"

"What would make you believe, Daniel?" Kathryn cried.

"I have to have proof that God exists."

"Like a miracle or something?"

"I dunno. I guess so. Why should anyone believe anything if there is no proof for it?"

"Stop being cynical. There are miracles all around us. Life is a wonderful miracle. Your very own life is a miracle. Look at everything surrounding us. Everything is so intricate, and it all fits together perfectly. God created this for us."

"I have a an argument on that comment; it's called the Big Bang Theory."

"So I guess evolution seems logical to you too?" Kathryn trailed off sarcastically.

"Don't be rude to me. I see no foundation for your argument either."

"No foundation? What do you think the Bible is?"

"Lots of people write books."

"Books? This is the Bible. There are facts in this book recorded over periods of years. People recorded those stories as they experienced them first-hand. They are *not* made up! So many miracles occurred and God and Jesus spoke to so many people. If it were made up, which it is not, there wouldn't be hundreds of people telling their related experiences. God spoke to those people so that one day we would know the love He felt for all mankind."

"One man could have written the whole thing."

"You're not being very open to what I'm trying to say. The very meaning of life is to exalt God!"

"What if I just don't want to hear it? Too many people disagree on the subject of religion and the meaning of life for one sure thing to be true. God is not a sure thing. No one has seen him. He isn't on any informative videos or anything."

"Stop trying to be funny! Just because people disagree about God, that doesn't make Him subjective."

"What? Okay, you lost me."

"Sorry, we just discussed this in Philosophy last week."

"Oh, gosh."

"What I mean to say is that just because you cannot touch or feel something—just because something is not objective—doesn't mean that that something is not true. We cannot touch or see our love, can we?"

“No, but at least I can touch you and know that I feel love between us, when we hug or kiss.”

“You are missing the point, Daniel. I am not *love*. When I walk by a crowd of people, they don’t point and say, ‘Look! It’s Love!’ or, ‘Can’t you see the love around her?’ It’s an analogy: You cannot touch God just like you cannot touch love. Just because we cannot touch or see love doesn’t mean that it isn’t real, and the same holds true for God.”

“I feel like you are trying to force me to believe in God.”

“My goodness, we’re not talking about cake. I’m not stuffing it down your throat. I just love you and find it very sad that you do not believe in God.”

“Fine. Now it is my turn to get my point across.”

“Shoot.”

“First and foremost, if there is a God, why is there evil in the world? Killing, shooting, lying, stealing . . .”

“Adam and Eve,” Kathryn interrupted.

“That is such crap. Just because of two people our world is cursed? And what about all of those innocent children that die every year? They don’t deserve to die. Shouldn’t God take care of them?”

“God does take care of them. He has a plan for their lives. They will spend all eternity in Heaven with him.”

“Whatever! Try and explain that to their parents. ‘Sorry, buddy, your kid’s with me in the clouds.’”

“Heaven.”

“Sorry, heaven.”

“That is just what I believe.”

“See, that brings up another point. So many people have so many opinions about what God does or what he likes.”

"Once again, that does not make it subjective."

"The way I see it is that we live our lives, we have fun, make mistakes, learn from them, and then die."

"Ah. Well, explain this, then: where do you get your conscience?"

"It's a learned trait. You learn after being punished a few times that you don't do certain things."

"Well, who started it?"

"I don't know, nor do I care."

"Fine, then. God instilled it in us," Kathryn said under her breath.

"Oh, and it seems that all believers say that God is everywhere and that he is watching everyone. That's really believable!"

"He *is* watching everyone! He is almighty; He watches over each and every one of us. He loves us." Daniel looked up at the sky and waved sarcastically.

"Am I making fun of *your* beliefs?"

"You're challenging them."

"Well, I am sorry, honey, but that is part of debating."

"The way I see it is that people believe what they want to believe. Whatever you believe is true for you."

"Well, maybe, but I am just so sorry that I didn't know about this sooner. All those times . . ."

"Well, I am not going to apologize if that's what you are fishing for. I shouldn't have to apologize for what I believe."

"I agree. I am just saying that I feel sorry for you."

"What are you so upset, Kathryn?"

"Because I love you. Just because bad things have happened to you doesn't mean that there is no God. Bad things happen to everyone."

"I love you too, Kathryn, but we are getting nowhere. I don't want to talk about this. That is why I never brought it up before, because I knew it would start a huge conflict. I *am* sorry, though, for not telling you the truth."

"You can't just avoid conflict. You are cheating yourself out of discovering something that might make sense to you."

"Maybe, but for right now, I'd rather not discuss it any more." He reached down, put the key in the ignition, and started the truck. Kathryn leaned over and kissed him on the cheek, and he pulled her into a hug.

She smiled and pulled away. "Daniel, I sympathize with you and why you may believe what you believe. We will stop talking about it for now, but this conversation is far from over."

Daniel laughed and said, "Maybe someday I will find a reason to believe, but for right now, things are looking pretty grim."

They drove home, considering their argument and wondering about the future of their lives together.